THE SYSTEM GAMBIT

Find Leverage to Unlock Compounding Value

RITAVAN

Award-Winning Author of DATA IMPACT

First published in 2026 by Bavarian Tiger Ventures GmbH.

Paperback ISBN: 978-3-9828972-1-9
eBook ISBN: 978-3-9828972-0-2

First Edition

10 9 8 7 6 5 4 3 2 1

To my readers who bring out the best in me,

---

and to Moutoshi,
for our greatest system gambit.

"This book captures one of the hardest truths about innovation: companies are rarely disrupted because they are incompetent. More often, they are disrupted because they are exceptionally good at playing yesterday's game. The idea of the system gambit offers a powerful lens to understand when leaders must stop optimizing current metrics and start building a new system of advantage. Clear, provocative, and deeply relevant, this is a valuable read for anyone who wants to lead transformation rather than merely react to it."

— Prof. Daniel Trabucchi, Professor at Politecnico di Milano; co-author of *Platform Thinking* and *The Digital Phoenix Effect*

"When I was asked to preview *The System Gambit*, I planned to skim it. I read it cover to cover instead. Ritavan pulls together history and mental models in a way that leaves you both wiser and itching to put them to work."

— Gary Mishuris, Managing Partner & CIO at Silver Ring Value Partners

"Taking a risk in your personal life is scary. Taking a risk in business, when you have employees, investors, and customers depending on you, can be even scarier. The System Gambit illustrates that taking a risk and shifting to a new system paradigm is often essential. Sticking with the status quo can put your business on the fast track to irrelevance. *The System Gambit* teaches readers when and how to make a system altering pivot that can save your business and set it up for years of success."

— Daryl Fairweather, Chief Economist at Redfin; author of *Hate the Game*

"I've believed for the past several years that AI's greatest advantages won't arise from what it automates and commoditizes, but from the age-old gaps between map and terrain that AI is fundamentally reshaping. Ritavan's *The System Gambit* is the philosophical and systematic unpacking that insight desperately needed. This is required reading for anyone building or investing in real value as every standardized task is commoditized."

— Matt Zeigler, Managing Director at Sunpointe Investments

"*The System Gambit* names what I've instinctively been doing in production for years while building AI systems that transform how the business runs. Its deep gift is the language and mental model to defend the move in the rooms where decisions actually get made."

— **Dr. Dora Simroth, Data & AI Executive**

" I have spent twenty-five years watching institutions optimise for what is measurable and politically safe: running the system anti-gambit by default.

The adoption gap and the governance gap are the same failure, institutions surrendering long-term structural advantage to protect locally optimal positions. This book gave me language for something I had observed but never clearly named.

The compounding is structural. The gap widens not because others work harder, but because the feedback loops never start. Most operators—in boardrooms and in government—never make the move."

— **Ratul Ahmed, Risk Management Executive**

"Ritavan's strength as an author is that each insight naturally raises the next question, which he then answers with the next piece of the framework. The result is a book whose structure reinforces its message. His concept of the System Anti-Gambit (the near miss that lacks a key ingredient) helps you internalize what makes a true System Gambit work.

Most valuable, though, is the pattern recognition the book will develop in you. Ritavan gives you the language and mental models for that meeting where everyone is agreeing to fund an initiative that is fine but will never create a lasting advantage. He describes that meeting so vividly that you'll recognize it immediately. It's obvious he's been there."

— **Lou Franco, author of *Swimming in Tech Debt***

TABLE OF CONTENTS

TABLE OF CONTENTS

TABLE OF CONTENTS

FOREWORD

I am a banker, not a historian, and also, I have never commanded an army, run an empire, or written a line of software. So when Ritavan asked me to introduce a book that travels from the dynasties of ancient China to the technology of Silicon Valley—by way of warlords, admirals, scientists, and the merchants of the medieval Baltic—I wondered what on earth I could write.

Then I read it, and recognised, in century after century and on continent after continent, the very dilemma that has occupied eleven generations of my own family: how does anything good last?

It is a peculiar feature of success that it plants the seeds of its own undoing.

The stratagem that carries you to the top hardens, in time, into dogma. The habits that once set you apart become the very things everyone else now does too. And the cleverer and more profitable your formula, the more reluctant you are to abandon it when the world undeniably changes underneath you. I have watched a good many organisations die of precisely this. They did not fail because they stopped doing what had worked. They failed precisely because they kept doing it.

Ritavan's insight, which he frames as *The System Gambit*, is that the organisations which endure are those willing to make a deliberate sacrifice: to give up something that looks valuable today in order to build the structural conditions that compounds tomorrow. It is a profoundly uncomfortable idea, because every instinct, every incentive, and every well-meaning adviser will counsel you against it. I know this, because my own generation has made such system gambits.

For example, a decade ago we sold our investment-management business, a perfectly good and viable enterprise, so that we could concentrate everything on the core of what we do. To some it looked like a retreat. It was in fact the opposite, because it eliminated the distraction.

Since then our banking business has compounded more strongly than I had dared hope. Einstein said compound interest is the eighth wonder of the world; but you only enjoy it if you are still in the game, and staying in the game sometimes means letting go of something you are rather proud of.

The book also argues, something I have long believed: that you must play to your own asymmetric strengths and attend to what genuinely matters to your customers instead of what your competitors announce they are doing. We have never tried to beat larger banks at scale or on price, at which they would crush us; we compete instead on relationship, judgement, humanity, and a kind of deep empathy that is not quantifiable on a quarterly earnings report.

A great deal of what passes for strategy in our industry is, I am afraid, often groupthink dressed up as "best practices", and we have consistently, and quite knowingly, ignored it. The herd offers comfort. But it rarely offers an advantage.

I insist that one must hold fast to one's mission and values while being open-minded about everything else. In our own case the processes have changed beyond all recognition over three and a half centuries, but the essence has not changed at all.

Our mission is simply to perpetuate a profitable family business, and to be good bankers and good citizens while we do it. Everything else, every procedure, every assumption, every tool, is fair game, and ought to be examined as though your survival depended upon it, because one day it will.

Which brings me to the question that now keeps my partners and me suitably awake at night: what will artificial intelligence mean for us? I confess I do not yet know. But I take real comfort from this book, because it offers not a forecast but a different way of thinking.

My own suspicion is that whatever an algorithm can most easily copy will swiftly become cheap, and that what will go on compounding is precisely what it cannot copy: trust built across generations, the judgement of people who actually know their customers, and a reputation that takes years to earn and an evening to lose. If I am right, the future will reward the very things our family has been successively accumulating since 1672, but I would not bet the bank on my being right, and that, I think, is rather Ritavan's point.

This is a learned, humane, pluripotent and genuinely provocative book about the oldest problem there is—*how to endure*—and it grasps what most strategy books never do: that endurance is not standing still, but the far harder discipline of changing everything except what matters most.

The question it poses has outlasted dynasties and empires, and all but a handful of the businesses that ever opened their doors; it will outlast our own age of artificial intelligence too. Few of us will build something that lasts more than three and a half centuries. But every one of us must decide, now, what we are willing to give up today, to unlock a structural advantage, so that what we value might still be compounding long after we are gone.

Alexander Hoare
Senior Partner of C. Hoare & Co
Author of *Impact Banker*

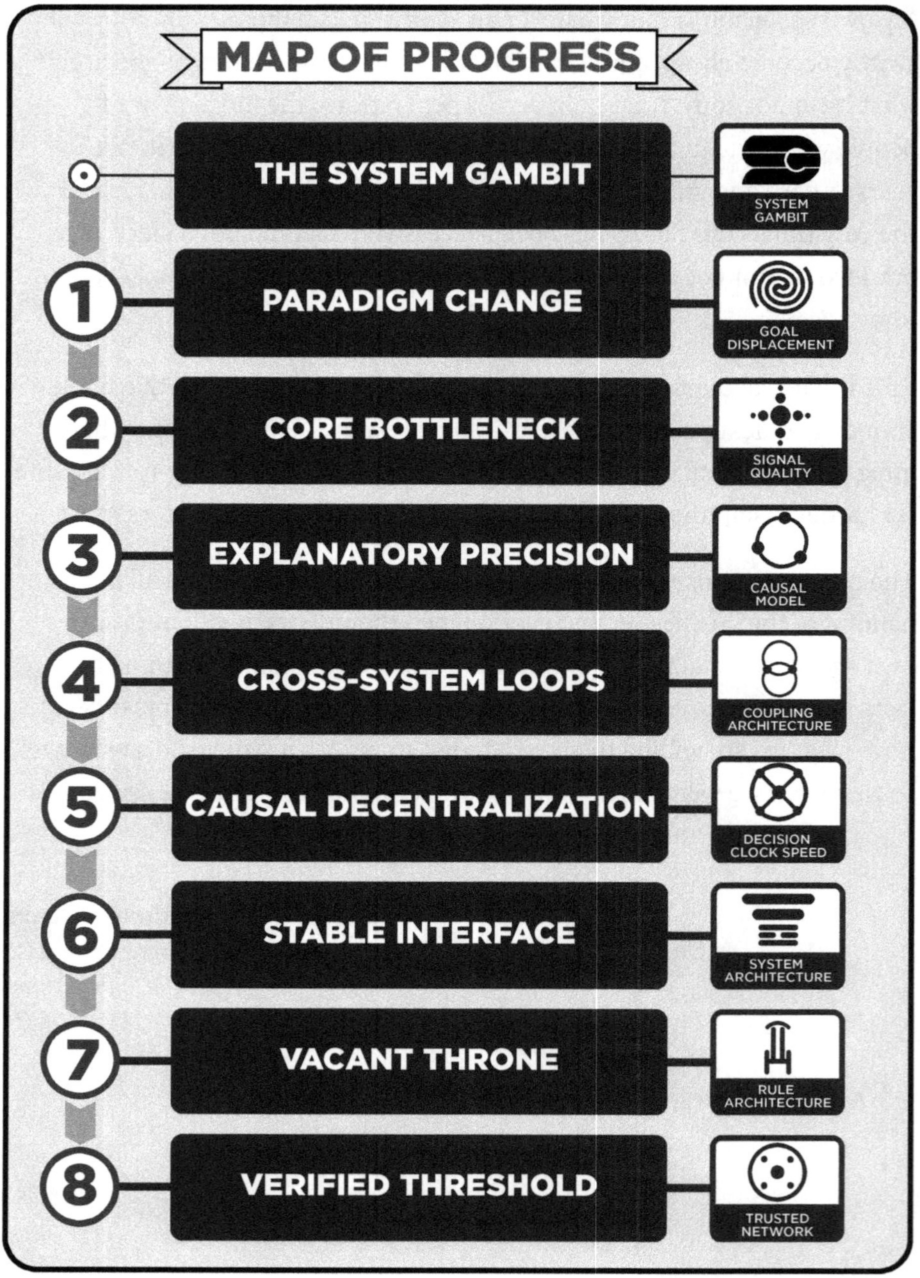
MAP OF PROGRESS
THE SYSTEM GAMBIT
SYSTEM GAMBIT
1
PARADIGM CHANGE
GOAL DISPLACEMENT
2
CORE BOTTLENECK
SIGNAL QUALITY
3
EXPLANATORY PRECISION
CAUSAL MODEL
4
CROSS-SYSTEM LOOPS
COUPLING ARCHITECTURE
5
CAUSAL DECENTRALIZATION
DECISION CLOCK SPEED
6
STABLE INTERFACE
SYSTEM ARCHITECTURE
7
VACANT THRONE
RULE ARCHITECTURE
8
VERIFIED THRESHOLD
TRUSTED NETWORK

THE SYSTEM GAMBIT

IN BRIEF

- In chess, a gambit is a move where material is surrendered in the beginning to eventually gain a compensating advantage that is structurally superior. This is the essential logic: sacrifice something measurable now to build something structural that generates compounding returns over time.
- A system gambit is the deliberate sacrifice of a locally optimal position—usually something currently valued, measurable, and visible—in order to build a specific structural condition that generates compounding advantage over time through feedback loops that the sacrificed position would have foreclosed.
- The system anti-gambit is not a mistake. It is the rational, locally optimal response to the current system's goals and metrics. That is why most operators run the system anti-gambit by default.
- The sacrifice is real: a measurable and painful drop in current system performance, and the abandoning of the management logic that produced it. It cannot be made incrementally.
- The compounding is structural: the gap widens every iteration not because the person executing the system gambit works harder, but because self-improving feedback loops run in the new system, that those outside the new system cannot replicate.
- Three conditions distinguish a genuine system gambit from a good investment: self-improvement, path-dependence, and management logic antagonism. All three must be present simultaneously.

Yi Sun-sin was appointed commander of the Left Naval Forces of Jeolla Province in early 1591. The threat of a Japanese invasion was already apparent to the people paying attention at court. Most Korean military planners were thinking about how to defend the peninsula. Yi was thinking about something different.

Japan could land about 160,000 men on the Korean coast. Japan could also march them north and capture every major city on the peninsula. By the late Sengoku period, around 1590, a unified Japan under Toyotomi Hideyoshi had built a brutal, coordinated military machine capable of successfully invading Korea. But 160,000 men in Korea could not eat local food indefinitely, could not carry Japanese ammunition across the sea in their pockets, and thus could definitely not survive without regular and uninterrupted resupply.

Every Japanese soldier on Korean soil was viable only as long as Japanese ships could reach Korean ports. The supply line was the binding constraint. Yi built this clear causal model, while virtually no one else in the Korean military leadership did so.

The painful sacrifice for Yi was land. While every other Korean commander framed the defence of cities and roads as the key to success, Yi saw it as a distraction from the only constraint governing the entire Japanese invasion. In May 1592, about 158000 Japanese forces landed and captured the capital in just 20 days. Every Korean military commander was heroically fighting the land war within the paradigm that had always governed Korean defence, and they were losing miserably and catastrophically within it. Yi let them fight that war. He was fighting a different one.

What Yi built during that year of preparation was designed for a single purpose: to prevent Japanese ships from resupplying Japanese soldiers. He built the panokseon warship with superior cannon range. He built the kobukseon, the so-called turtle ship, as a lethal weapon for disruption and ramming. He also built an intelligence network of coastal informants.

Each supply convoy he destroyed weakened Japanese land forces fighting deeper in the peninsula. Degraded land forces forced the Japanese to concentrate naval protection around the remaining supply routes. This made Japanese ship movements even more predictable. That predictability made Yi even more lethal, allowing him to identify vulnerable convoys and destroy successive fleets with fewer resources than before. Each cycle made the next cycle more effective.

By the autumn of the same year, the Japanese land advance had stalled. This had little to do with the Korean land army, which continued to get decimated, and so it had everything to do with Japanese soldiers at the front beginning to run out of supplies and starve.

Then Yi's own king had him arrested. It is rumoured that political rivals at court, coordinating with Japanese double agents, convinced the king that Yi had disobeyed orders. He was imprisoned, tortured, and stripped of command. His replacement, Won Kyun, took the massive 166 ship fleet Yi had built through years of preparation and destroyed practically all of it in a single incompetent naval engagement. The Japanese resumed their resupply, and the land war recommenced in full force.

Yi was eventually reinstated as Supreme Commander. The Japanese armada that had destroyed Won Kyun's Joseon fleet, now numbered somewhere between 120 and 333 warships, depending on the historical source you pick. The Korean king wrote to Yi, suggesting he abandon the navy altogether and fight on land. Yi wrote back that he still had 13 ships and would continue to fight at sea.

He chose his naval battleground at the Myeongnyang Strait. The strait was only about 300 metres wide, with tidal currents reversing every few hours. Yi positioned his 13 ships across the channel and patiently waited. When the Japanese armada entered, the narrow waterway negated their numerical advantage, just as it had done for the large Persian army when they faced the 300 Spartans at Thermopylae. The tidal reversal broke the Japanese formation at a critical moment in the battle. Thirty-one Japanese warships were sunk or disabled. Not a single Korean ship was lost.

The painful sacrifice Yi made was a full year before the successful battle in the strait that day. Yi's sacrifice began when he chose the management logic of constraint-level naval resupply denial, while every commander who outranked him was competing on the metrics of land-based territorial defence. Yi was not at all interested in fighting the current war better, instead, he was obsessed with fighting the only war that would determine the decisive outcome he wanted: the end of the entire Japanese invasion.

Yi died winning his last battle in 1598, struck by a musket ball as the Japanese finally withdrew. His reported last words were a request that his death be concealed from his troops until the battle was over. In his entire life, Yi never lost a battle. He never fully recovered his king's trust. He never received, in his lifetime, the recognition that what he had built was the reason Korea still exists today.

The three-question system gambit test asks whether the sacrifice was real, whether the structural condition was clear, and whether the compounding logic existed. Yi's sacrifice was brutally real: he let cities fall while his superiors demanded he defend them, and he was even imprisoned for it. His structural condition was clear: the closed feedback loop between the destruction of resupply convoys and the degradation of the land force, running through naval control of the Korean straits. His compounding logic was robust: each destroyed convoy made the next one easier to find and more devastating if destroyed. All three were present. Yi's system gambit was complete.

What was absent was the institutional architecture to hold the system gambit in place after the person who made it was gone. The system gambit tells you what sacrifice to make and what structural condition to build. It does not guarantee that the organization you build it inside will automatically understand what you built, protect it when you are under attack, or sustain it when you are no longer there to defend it.

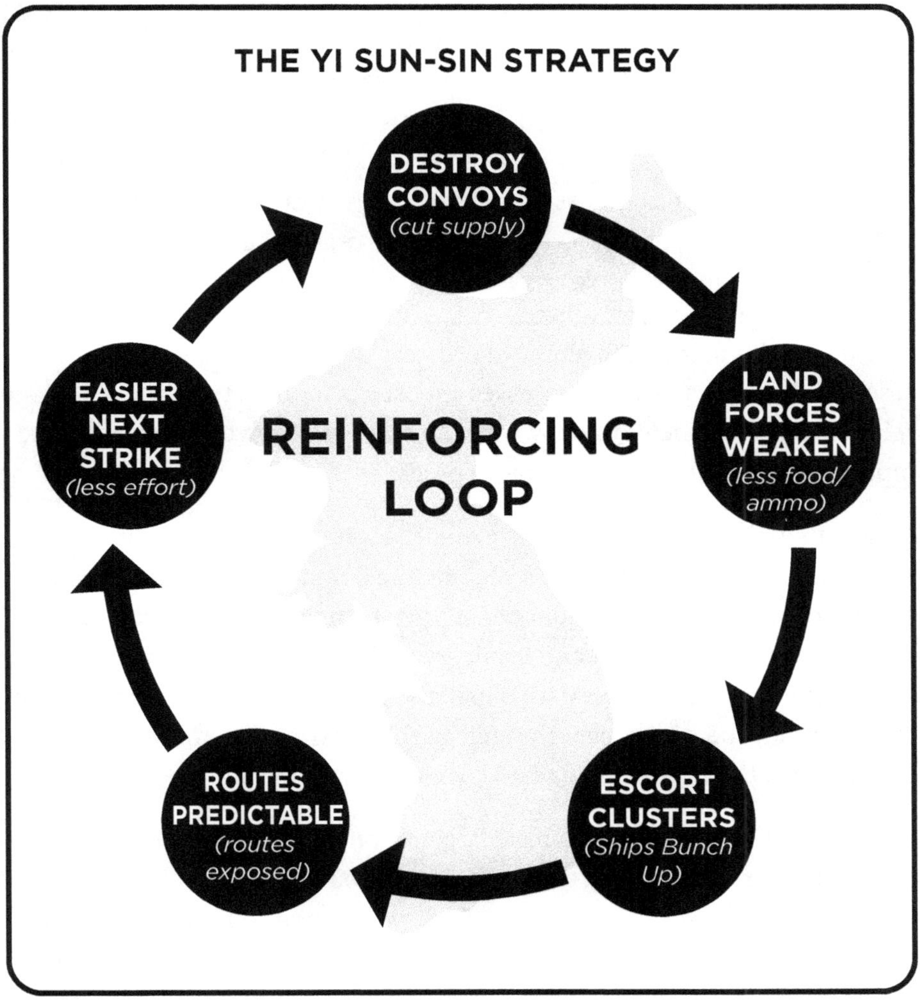

This is the essential structure of the system gambit. You sacrifice locally optimal performance in the current system, like for example the performance that present benchmarks measure, that current customers reward, or that current competitors imitate, to enter a different system whose architecture contains a self-reinforcing structural feedback loop that generates compounding returns the current system cannot access, and hence replicate.

> **THE SYSTEM GAMBIT**
> A system gambit is the deliberate abandonment of a locally optimal position in the current system, and the management logic that produced it, in order to enter a different system whose architecture contains a self-reinforcing structural feedback loop that generates compounding returns unavailable to operators who remain in the current system.

The keyword is **self-reinforcing**: an ordinary investment buys a better asset, while a system gambit accesses a feedback loop, a structural relationship in the new system where the output of each cycle becomes the input that makes the next cycle more productive.

Amazon's early investment in delivery speed was a bet that delivery speed, ease, and reliability would become the binding constraint on repeat purchase rates, and that a feedback loop between delivery performance and customer commitment and loyalty would compound faster than any competitor optimizing the existing metrics, even as selection breadth could match. It did, and by the time the shift in the criterion became visible to competitors, the compounding had been running for years.

What Yi Sun-sin and Amazon have in common is that neither improved the existing criterion. They were not simply doing what their competitors were doing, but just doing it better. They were doing something that their competitors' management logic—the logic that made those competitors successful in the current system—prevented them from doing. That prevention is structural and a durable moat because it is not a matter of will or intelligence. You cannot build a navy designed to starve an army while also defending the cities that the army is burning. The management logics are antagonistic and in direct conflict. Choosing one, by design, forecloses the other.

THE CURRENT SYSTEM	THE NEW SYSTEM
• Locally optimal • Measured • Rewarded by current benchmarks • Requires the management logic that makes you successful today	• Self-reinforcing loop • Not measured or visible so far • Requires a management logic that actively destroys the current one

What Makes It a Genuine System Gambit

Not every sacrifice results in a system gambit. Not every new system contains a self-reinforcing loop. Three conditions must hold simultaneously for something to be a system gambit. If any one of them fails, the result ceases to be a system gambit, because it becomes either a good investment (real returns without compounding), a speculative bet (uncertain returns without structural conditions), or simply a mistake.

CONDITION	WHAT IT MEANS	WHY IT FAILS WITHOUT IT
Self-improvement (the feedback loop condition)	Each cycle of the structural relationship makes the next cycle more productive without equivalent additional input.	You have bought a better asset. Returns are real but they do not compound. There is no loop.
Path-dependence (the irreversibility condition)	The advantage cannot be replicated by entering the new system later with more resources. Replication requires running the loop from the beginning.	A late entrant can simply invest to match you. The moat is real but it does not compound.
Management logic antagonism (the sacrifice condition)	The logic required to build the new system actively destroys the logic required to maintain the existing system. You cannot have both simultaneously.	The sacrifice is a resource allocation decision, not a system crossing. A genuine gambit requires that you cannot be on both axes at once.

The three conditions together produce the defining property of a system gambit: a compounding position that widens every period, not because you work harder but because the loop runs. The gap between the gambit-maker and the operator who remains in the current system grows with time, even if both work equally hard. This is the difference between linear returns and structural compounding.

Amazon's delivery commitment data loop generates one behavioural data point per fulfilled order. Each data point improves the prediction of what a customer will order next. Better prediction improves inventory placement. Better inventory placement improves delivery speed. Faster delivery generates more orders. More orders generate more data points. The loop: data → prediction → placement → speed → orders → data. Each cycle produces the input that makes the next cycle more accurate. A retailer outside this loop cannot replicate the compounding position, regardless of the scale of capital investment, because the compounding history cannot be purchased.

Why Most People Are in the System Anti-Gambit

Here is what makes the system gambit genuinely difficult, and why this book exists: the system anti-gambit is not a mistake. This locally optimal position is the correct answer to the question the current system is asking.

Your performance review measures your current-criterion capability. Your clients pay for your current-criterion expertise. Your industry rewards your current-criterion excellence. Your competitors are optimizing the current criterion. Every signal your environment generates is telling you the same thing: get better at what you are already good at. The management logic that makes you successful in the current system will, if you follow it consistently, make you the best possible version of an operator in the current system. That is right up to the moment the current system becomes irrelevant.

> ***The system anti-gambit is not a mistake. It is the rational, locally optimal response to the current system's metrics and management logic.***
>
> ***The trap is that the current system's rewards actively prevent you from seeing the sacrifice as anything other than a mistake.***

The same dynamic operates at every scale. The company that should be building a trusted, verified interaction history is instead maximizing user count, because investors measure user count, whereas trusted, verified interaction quality does not. The organization that should be distributing its causal model to operating units is instead centralizing decisions, because centralization produces the outcomes that performance reviews currently reward. The policymaker who should be occupying the rule-setting positions for AI governance is instead holding hearings, because hearings create a good show without changing much on the ground, and building governance infrastructure before the crisis is not even visible to voters. The management logic of the current system is, by default, always and everywhere, to select against the sacrifice the system's gambit requires.

The Sacrifice

The sacrifice is real. It is not a metaphor, not a clever reframing, or a savvy way of describing an investment that will pay off quickly in the short term. It is a deterioration in your current-criterion performance as you build the new system's structural condition. That non-negotiable pain is what makes the sacrifice real.

The sacrifice is real and, in a more important sense, very painful: the management logic required to build the new system actively destroys the management logic required to maintain the current one. You cannot maintain both industrial variance elimination and digital variance exploration simultaneously within the same management framework. You cannot simultaneously maximize inclusion speed and enforce verification rigour in the same onboarding process. You cannot centralize decision authority and distribute decision frequency simultaneously within the same governance structure.

> ***The sacrifice is not "invest less here to invest more there".***
>
> ***It is "abandon the logic that makes you successful in the current system, in order to build with the logic that makes the new system compound".***
>
> ***The two cannot coexist.***

This is why the system gambit cannot be made incrementally. You cannot edge towards the new system while maintaining your position in the current one. The management logic antagonism prevents it. Every half-measure produces the worst of both: the current system's performance degraded by the distraction of building the new system, and the new system's structural condition never reaches the threshold required for compounding to begin. The organizations that try to run both together produce neither outcome. This is a structural consequence of attempting a genuine system gambit without making the genuine sacrifice.

The Compounding

Once the sacrifice has been made and the structural condition has been built, something changes that cannot be undone by the competitors remaining in the current system: the loop begins to compound.

The compounding is not primarily financial, though financial returns eventually materialize; rather, it is fundamentally structural. Each cycle of the self-reinforcing feedback loop makes the next cycle more effective. Toyota's production learning loop generates one insight per production run. Each insight improves the next production run. The improved production run yields more refined insights. The loop runs faster than any competitor outside it can match.

This path-dependence is the third dimension of the system gambit's power. It means that the advantage is both temporary and structurally durable in ways that ordinary competitive advantages rarely are. A better product can be copied. A better process can be licensed. A better team can be hired away. No amount of investment can replicate a compounding loop that has been running for five years, because replication requires five years of loop operation, which cannot be magically created; it can only be built over 5 years.

> ***The gap does not stay constant. It widens every period, not because the system gambit investor-operator works harder, but because the loop generates its own improvement. The competitor who stays in the current system falls further behind with each cycle of a loop they are not inside.***

This is the compounding that the rest of this book delivers: eight distinct types of self-reinforcing structural relationships exist in complex systems. Each generates a different kind of compounding. Each requires a different type of sacrifice to access. Each has a specific system genre of system anti-gambit, the locally optimal position that forecloses the structural condition, that most operators are running right now, rationally, correctly, but within the logic of the system they are in.

The eight-system anti-gambits are introduced in the following chapters, from the most widely experienced to the most structurally invisible. You will recognize the first one immediately. It will feel like your own lived experience described with strange familiarity. By the time you reach the eighth system gambit, the key question will be which of these system anti-gambits you are currently running, and what, specifically, the sacrifice would require to cross to the other side.

What the System Gambit Is Not

The system gambit is not a call to reckless disruption. Not every existing system should be abandoned. Not every new system contains a compounding loop. Most "disruptions" are not system gambits: they are bets on improvements within the existing system's logic, deceitfully dressed in the language of "transformation".

The test is rigorous: does the new system contain a structural relationship that self-improves, that is path-dependent, and whose management logic is genuinely antagonistic to the management logic that produced your current success?

If any of these conditions fails, the outcome ceases to qualify as a system gambit. It becomes either a good investment or a mistake.

The system gambit is not a permanent sacrifice. The sacrifice is the entry cost, not the ongoing cost forever. Once the structural condition has been built and the loop is running, the system gambit investor–operator is in the new system, and the sacrifice period is over. What follows is compounding, which is not sacrifice, but the reward for the sacrifice that was already made at the outset.

The system gambit is not a guarantee either. The path-dependence cuts both ways. If you make the sacrifice and the structural condition never reaches the threshold required for compounding to begin, then you will have lost the current-system position without gaining the new-system compounding. The system gambit requires both a sacrifice and the correct identification of the loop. Both are difficult, and neither can be fully de-risked. What the system gambit framework provides isn't simplistic certainty, but instead it gives you rigorous clarity about what is necessary.

In a chess gambit, sacrifice and gain occur within the same system. Because both players are playing chess, the advantage is a better chess position. In the business world, the most powerful gambits happened across systems. The sacrifice is made in one system. The compounding gains are located in a completely different system, one with a different management logic, different metrics, and a self-reinforcing structural feedback loop that the first system cannot access at all.

In chess, the best players do not make gambits because they love risk. They make gambits because they have calculated that the positional advantage

> A system gambit is the deliberate abandonment of a locally optimal position in the current system, and the management logic that produced it, in order to enter a different system whose architecture contains a self-reinforcing structural feedback loop that generates compounding returns.
> The irreversibility arises because the new system does not exist in the current system that was abandoned: competitors who retained the locally optimal position are not behind in the same race, they are in a structurally different system where the new system's compounding loop is absent.

they will gain is worth more than the material they will lose, and because they understand, better than their opponents, what kind of advantage compounds and what kind does not.

The same opportunity is available to you, and this book will show you how you can pivot from the system anti-gambit to the system gambit to win big.

GAMBIT ONE

GOAL DISPLACEMENT: PARADIGM CHANGE

Goal Displacement: Paradigm Change

In the mid-sixteenth century, Japan was not the unified country it is today. It was more of a fragmented chessboard, each piece engaged in brutal civil war: 200-250 fiefdoms, each ruled by a daimyo warlord. Economic power was measured in koku, the quantity of rice needed to feed one person for one year. The major clans controlled territories that produced between

300,000 and 1,000,000 koku annually, which translated directly into armies of 20,000 to 50,000 warriors, illustrating how economic and military power were often underwritten by the same currency: koku.

The large Hōjō clan controlled the agriculturally rich Kantō plain in eastern Japan, and their dominance was built on land productivity. Neighbouring them to the west, the Takeda clan ruled over the rich gold mines of Kai province, and built a legendary cavalry, composed of not just traditional mounted samurai archers, but signature mounted shock lancers who could break enemy formations in the first minutes of engagement. To their north was the Uesugi clan, whose domains combined fertile rice cultivation with control over critical trade routes and the lucrative salt trade. This allowed the Uesugi to field large armies.

In the west, the Mōri controlled 10 provinces, access to the Seto Inland Sea trade routes, iron ore deposits, and a naval force and army large enough to back their territorial ambitions across land and sea simultaneously. The Ōtomo, further south-west, built their power through major international ports and the overseas commerce that flowed through them. And finally, to the south, the Shimazu clan ruled a relatively remote province but was famous for a fierce military culture that produced warriors the other clans feared.

Somewhere in the middle of this complex and charged chessboard was Owari province: small, landlocked, and home to the Oda clan. When daimyo Oda Nobuhide, the "Tiger of Owari", died in 1551, his eldest son, Oda Nobunaga, inherited a province that had no gold mines, no salt monopoly, no naval routes, no outsized agricultural base, and no international trade access. But what Owari province had just gained was a maverick leader with a special eye and disposition towards problems that could not be solved by conventional means.

In 1543, about eight years before Nobunaga started consolidating his control over the Oda clan, a Chinese junk trading ship anchored off Tanegashima, a thin, elongated island south of the main Japanese archipelago. Tanegashima is so small that one can ride across its entire length in a day. Interestingly, the storm that had battered the ship also altered the trajectory of Japanese history, though no one on the island knew it yet. Among the passengers of the junk were two Portuguese adventurers carrying objects no one in all of Japan had ever seen before: a pair of front-loading matchlock arquebuses.

Tanegashima Tokitaka, the young daimyo of the island, was what we would today call a tech enthusiast: young, curious, forward-looking, and passionate about technical detail. He purchased both firearms immediately and tasked his master swordsmith, Yaita Kinbei Kiyosada, with disassembling and replicating them. The talented swordsmith succeeded in replicating every component except one: the screw threads required for the firing mechanism. Japan had threaded pottery, but it lacked precision threading in metal. The following year, Tokitaka brought in a Portuguese blacksmith and solved the problem conclusively.

Within a few years, production centres had emerged across Japan. In Sakai and Kunitomo, artisans manufactured firearms with calibres standardized to a degree unprecedented in either Europe or China at the time: a manufacturing discipline that would prove to be one of the gun's most consequential hidden properties. Recent radiological analysis of Tanegashima guns has even revealed that firearms produced using Japanese sword-forging techniques contained fewer metal impurities, making them structurally more stable and more powerful than their Portuguese originals.

And yet for the next two decades, the Tanegashima gun appeared to be, by every measurable criterion, a total military failure. It lost in direct combat to every existing traditional weapon. Against the yumi bow, the asymmetric composite longbow that had dominated Japanese warfare for centuries, the gun's inferiority was shockingly obvious.

A skilled samurai archer could lose 10 to 15 arrows in the time it took a gunner to reload and fire once. The gun's accuracy was inferior, and more worryingly, it was unreliable in high-humidity weather and entirely inoperable in rain. These were all conditions the yumi handled without any degradation in performance. When early adopters added gunners to traditional samurai units, combat performance dropped drastically. The smoke and noise disrupted unit cohesion. The reload delays created gaps that disciplined archer formations never had.

The formidable Hōjō, Takeda, Uesugi, Mōri, and other clans assessed the Tanegashima gun analytically and reached the same rational conclusion. The Tanegashima gun might be useful in special, controlled situations, but it was definitely not appropriate for mainstream military use. A new technology tool, to be handled carefully by trained experts, without any serious plan for how to deploy it in a real battle. In corporate vocabulary, they ran pilot projects, with no clear view of how to create impact at scale in production.

> ***The major clans weren't wrong about what the new technology could do.***
>
> ***But they were shockingly wrong about the system gambit the new technology gave rise to.***

The established yumi bow benchmarks for per-shot accuracy, reload speed, weather reliability, and effectiveness in individual combat were not arbitrary. They had been refined and optimized over centuries of samurai warfare because they measured precisely what determined success in that paradigm.

The samurai system was built on individual valour: small, autonomous units in which personal contribution could be observed, attributed, and ritually confirmed. The kubi jiken ceremony, in which the cleaned and decorated heads of defeated opponents were formally identified and attributed to specific warriors, was a gruesome custom that effectively served as the samurai warfare paradigm's performance-review mechanism.

Status, advancement, and the entire social architecture of the warrior class were organized around individually measurable martial contribution. The yumi bow amplified individual skill, because years of dedicated training produced archers who could deliver sustained, accurate, weather-resistant arrow fire. Every benchmark the samurai paradigm used was calibrated to detect bow-like advantages, since they were exactly what the battlefield had rewarded over centuries.

The Tanegashima gun failed those benchmarks precisely because it was irrelevant to individual skill. A motivated peasant with three weeks of training could fire a Tanegashima gun with lethality matching that of a skilled samurai. This was a brazen insult to the paradigm's logic of leadership and management.

Here is the structural advantage that the powerful Hōjō, Takeda, Uesugi, and Mōri military commanders could not see: the gun's unique asymmetric edge lay in standardized mass production, low individual training costs, and, most importantly, the capacity for concentrated, coordinated, continuous firepower. All of these advantages were invisible to samurai paradigm benchmarks because those unique asymmetric advantages existed only in a new paradigm that had not yet emerged on the battlefield. This new paradigm would be a system organized around collective coordinated mass effects rather than individual martial excellence.

> ***You can only measure the performance of a new tech tool on existing paradigm benchmarks, but you can't measure its performance in a new paradigm designed around its new asymmetric advantages, because that paradigm does not yet exist.***

This is the nature of every paradigm shift: the benchmarks of the current paradigm are not measuring the wrong thing by accident or incompetence. They are measuring the right thing for the goals and constraints they were originally designed to detect. The problem is that new technology moves the decisive criteria, and accurate measurement instruments pointed at an irrelevant target produce plausible-looking but entirely useless readings.

In That Meeting

You have sat in this meeting: the presentation is about adopting a new technology. The slide deck shows adoption timelines, implementation milestones, and ROI projections over three years. One person describes what a competitor is doing, and another cites an analyst report claiming that all white-collar jobs will disappear next year. The numbers and narrative are spun into a smooth corporate slogan, and everyone pretends to nod along. And yet you sense unease in the room; in fact, that unease is coming from deep down inside you.

The question that isn't being asked is whether the benchmarks in the ROI model are measuring the right thing. Whether the metrics being used to evaluate the new technology were designed to detect the unique asymmetric advantages of this new technology. Your unease is justified because buying and naïvely adopting new technology based on ROI projections of benchmarks that can be competed away in the existing paradigm is a pure waste of resources.

Charlie Munger diagnosed this trap in a 1994 talk at USC Business School. When Berkshire's textile mills were presented with a new loom that was twice as efficient, Warren Buffett said he hoped they wouldn't work, because if they did, he'd sell the mill. Not because the loom was bad technology, but because the relevant question was never what the technology could do. The relevant question was whether the system they were operating within would allow them to retain the benefits of the new technology.

In a commoditized industrial business, they would keep none of the gains, because any efficiency gains would eventually flow through competitive pricing straight to customers. The asymmetric advantage of the new loom belonged up front to the seller of the new looms, and eventually to the buyers of the finished textiles, not to the mill owners who bought the machines.

Munger observed that every capital expenditure proposal he saw contained one step of the analysis, that this equipment will pay for itself in just a few years, while simultaneously omitting the second step entirely: how much of that saving stays inside the business, and how much gets competed away.

In a commodity system, practically all of it gets competed away. So you buy the first tech tool, then the next one, and after 20 years of naïve adoption of the most cutting-edge tech tools, your ROI remains static at 4% per annum. In the best case, the cutting-edge tech tool might have delivered exactly what it promised, but your business captured no additional value from it. In the worst case, you got conned into buying shiny bling-bling trash that is worthless for your business.

The contrast Munger drew completes the argument: install the same new technology at the only newspaper in a city (obviously pre-internet), and every dollar of efficiency gain flows to the bottom line: same cutting-edge tech tool, but opposite outcome. The difference lies not in the tool itself, but it lies in the system's structural position for deploying it. Pricing power means efficiency compounds as return on investment. Commodity competition means efficiency compounds, resulting in lower prices for customers and higher revenues for whoever sold you the equipment.

> ***The capability of a new technology is a property of the tool. Whether you are better off at the end is a property of the system and paradigm you operate in.***

Naïve tech adoption answers the first question and never asks the second. If every competitor can buy the same tool and deploy it within the same paradigm, the efficiency gains might be real, yet the competitive compounding gains are zero.

Even before firearms reached Japan, Oda Nobunaga had already demonstrated an unusual capacity for a pragmatic, first-principles systems rethink. Where conventional samurai doctrine favoured short spears of around 270 centimetres for individual combat, Nobunaga standardized longer spears of 360 centimetres and up to 700 centimetres, and then organized non-samurai ashigaru peasant units into compact three-row formations called yaribusuma, or "spear walls".

This was a double paradigm break: the physical innovation of longer spears in a disciplined formation negated the cavalry-charge advantage of clans with much larger armies, and the social innovation of hiring and promoting peasants on merit rather than lineage broke the assumption that military capability was a property of birth. His top general, Toyotomi Hideyoshi, would go on to become the first person to unify Sengoku Japan: a peasant-turned-military commander-turned-apex leader of a conservative, lineage-based society.

Oda Nobunaga did not see the Tanegashima gun as a new technology; he saw it as a new opportunity to scale his yaribusuma system into units of continuous, coordinated, concentrated firepower. Where other daimyos measured the Tanegashima gun against yumi bow benchmarks and found them lacking, Nobunaga set those benchmarks aside and asked a different question: what system would need to exist for this new technology's unique asymmetric properties to become a compounding advantage?

Those properties had nothing to do with individual accuracy. Nobunaga identified three intrinsic superpowers of the gun that the prevailing paradigm lacked the framework to leverage successfully.

First: standardized mass production. The calibre standardization already emerging in Sakai and Kunitomo meant firearms could be produced at scale with interchangeable components, something the custom-crafted yumi bow, matched to each archer's body and technique, could never be. So Nobunaga made sure he controlled the supply chain and built proprietary production capability.

Second: low individual training cost. Where a yumi archer required years of rigorous physical conditioning to reach battlefield effectiveness, a gunner

CAPABILITIES	WEAPON
Range	
Rate of Fire	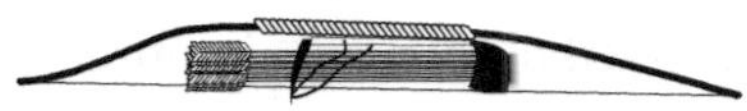
Accuracy	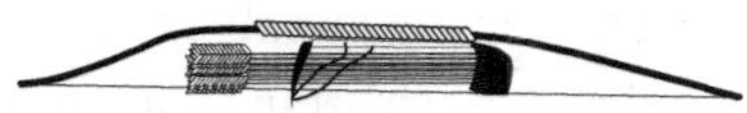
Reliability	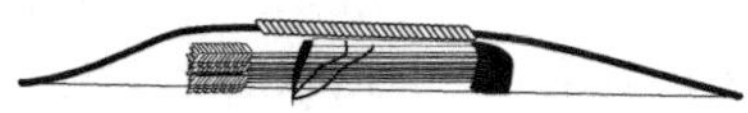
NEW CAPABILITIES	**WEAPON**
Range	
Rate of Fire	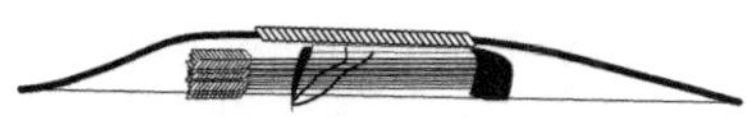
Accuracy	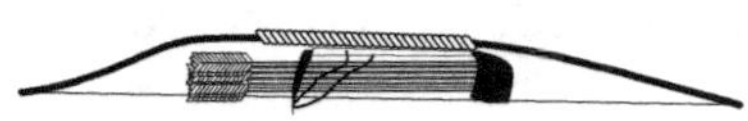
Reliability	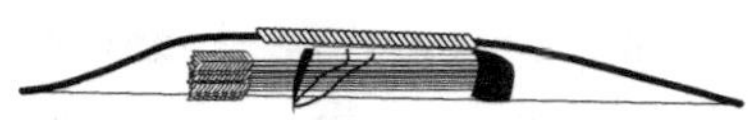
Armour Piercing	
Ease of Training	
Ability to Mass Produce	

could reach minimum functional competence in weeks. The constraint on army size was no longer the supply of hereditary warriors. It was ambitious people and reliable logistics. So Nobunaga recruited and promoted non-samurai soldiers based on merit and outcomes.

Third (***and the most important***)**:** the capacity for continuous, coordinated, concentrated firepower. A hundred archers were a hundred individuals firing. A hundred gunners, drilled in rotating volley sequences, were a single system producing sustained combined effects that no individual, however skilled, could replicate or withstand. And more importantly, you couldn't continuously fire a bow for more than a few minutes at a time because your arm muscles wouldn't allow you to, but loading and firing a gun was a lot less exhausting and thus more durable and scalable on the battlefield. Nobunaga had already proven this with spears; now, he did it with firearms.

Nobunaga moved on all these three fronts simultaneously. He designed multi-row ashigaru gunner units with rotating volley fire, enveloped by his existing yaribusuma spear wall formations, with the spears covering the guns' reload vulnerability, and the guns providing the sustained firepower the spears were incapable of generating. Where possible, he built reinforced wooden palisades to further protect his gunner units on the open battlefield.

He dominated the firearms supply chain by securing control of key ports, particularly Sakai, the primary production centre. And he standardized components and drilled ashigaru gunner units to a level of discipline that transformed individual valour and weapons into a reliable, coordinated killing machine.

At the Battle of Nagashino in 1575, just over two decades after the first firearms arrived in Japan, Nobunaga destroyed the feared Takeda cavalry and routed the entire Takeda army. Over the next decades, successes were further scaled by his general, Tokugawa Ieyasu, so that by the Battle of Sekigahara in 1600, historians estimate that more than 25,000 guns appeared on a single battlefield. By some accounts, Japan possessed more than half of the world's firearms by the end of the sixteenth century.

Let that sink in: the most traditional samurai culture simultaneously had the majority of guns.

The mechanism behind Oda Nobunaga's system gambit is what matters. And to understand what this means for your business, you need to understand not just that paradigms exist, but exactly how each one is built, what makes it irreconcilable with the others, and why deploying the tech tools of one paradigm within the management logic of another systematically caps your returns and prevents compounding of value.

SACRIFICE	STRUCTURAL CONDITION	COMPOUNDING LOGIC
Optimization on the current system's criterion: building capability towards what current benchmarks reward, what current customers expect, what current competitors compete on. This is the management logic of competitive excellence in the existing market.	A capability position advanced towards the future decisive criterion during the full period when competitors are still building for the current criterion. The structural condition is the accumulated capability gap: the gambit-maker is multiple investment cycles ahead on the criterion that will become decisive.	When the criterion shift occurs (driven by the gambit-maker's own investment, by technology, or by regulation), the gambit-maker is already compounding ahead. Competitors must change management logic and close the capability gap simultaneously. Each additional period of building widens both distances.

The Industrial Paradigm: The Process Is the Engine

The industrial paradigm is organized around a core binding constraint: a near-constant marginal cost of replication. Not which products to make. Not who wants them. But how many can be made, how reliably, and at what cost? Everything else flows from that core constraint.

The engine of value in the industrial paradigm is the repeatable process: the standardized, low-variance sequence of steps that converts inputs into outputs at predictable cost and quality.

The US Springfield Armory's shift in the early nineteenth century to interchangeable parts was not primarily a story about producing better muskets, as it might seem on first reading. It was a story about a new engine of value: once components were standardized to tight tolerances, repair became replacement, training became task execution, and output became a function of process discipline rather than personal craftsmanship.

The yumi bow was the weapon of the artisanal paradigm. The Tanegashima gun, standardized in Sakai and Kunitomo, was the industrial paradigm's weapon, not necessarily because it was more technically sophisticated, but because it could be produced, replicated, and deployed through processes rather than individual talent.

The industrial paradigm's goal is sustainable throughput at the governing constraint. Revenue and profit are downstream consequences of throughput. The binding question is always: what is the critical bottleneck, and how do we maximize flow through it without degrading it?

Improvements that matter are those that increase throughput, reduce variability at the bottleneck, or remove the bottleneck entirely, thereby shifting the constraint elsewhere in the system. These are the improvements that compound in value, and all impactful innovations focus on them. The industrial paradigm's feedback loops are stabilizing: they are designed to detect deviations from the process standard and correct them. Variation is not information in this system: variation is a defect.

A cement kiln that drifts 15 degrees outside its optimal temperature range doesn't produce slightly worse cement; it produces unusable output and creates downtime that cascades through every downstream process that depends on continuous feed. The entire management logic of the industrial paradigm, including lean manufacturing, Six Sigma, Theory of Constraints, and statistical process control, is organized around eliminating variance. You make the process reliable by detecting and eliminating variance before it propagates.

Scaling in the industrial paradigm is linearly related to physical capacity. You build another factory, hire more workers, and add another shift. Each additional unit of output requires additional physical inputs at roughly constant per-unit cost, bounded below by economies of scale and above by constraints on capital, labour, and logistics. Once you produce it at the lowest possible cost, any price above that cost is potentially pure profit.

The Digital Paradigm: The Validated Use Case Is the Engine

The digital paradigm starts when a new economic reality changes the binding constraint: when the marginal cost of replication collapses towards zero, production is no longer the constraint. A piece of software, an eBook, or a digital video, once produced, can be delivered to one user or 1 million users at essentially the same marginal cost. This single property changes everything about what an organization should optimize for.

When replication is free, the constraint shifts from how to produce to what is worth producing. The central question shifts from efficiency to discovery: which problems do real users actually have, under what conditions, and how reliably will they pay to have them solved? This cannot be answered through planning; it can only be answered through rigorous experimentation with real user behaviour.

The engine of value in the digital paradigm is the validated use case: a specific, recurring pattern of user behaviour that has been confirmed empirically through observed actions rather than assumed from a plan. Google did not win the search market because its algorithm was better. Numerous search engines had technically comparable algorithms by the early 2000s. Google won because it combined search with AdWords: converting each query into a real-time experiment on user intent and advertisers' willingness to pay, and using that experiment to improve the next. Each click tested relevance. Each conversion validated value. Each cycle made the next cycle more relevant.

While traditional advertising sold fixed inventory at negotiated prices, with feedback measured quarterly, AdWords ran millions of simultaneous experiments, with feedback measured in seconds and minutes. The engine of value was not the just the search result visible to the user, but the continuously self-improving loop between user intent and advertiser bids.

The digital paradigm's goal is to maximize the rate of validated learning: the speed at which the system converts uncertainty about what users want into confirmed behavioural evidence that they do want it. The binding question is always: how fast can we test a belief against real behaviour, and how quickly can we update our product in response?

Everything that slows this cycle, such as lengthy release processes, large batch sizes, and centralized approval chains, is a waste in the digital paradigm, even if it would be an excellent "best practice" in the industrial one.

The digital paradigm's feedback loops are accelerating: they are designed to amplify signals from user behaviour and feed them back into the product faster than competitors can. Variation is not a defect here. Variation is, in fact, the source of information. An A/B test that produces a failed variant hasn't wasted resources; it has eliminated a false belief and narrowed the envelope of uncertainty.

The management logic of the digital paradigm, characterized by rapid iteration, minimum viable products, continuous deployment, and behavioural instrumentation, is organized around exploring variance. You reduce uncertainty by deliberately introducing variation and rigorously measuring outcomes through a closed, reinforcing feedback loop.

Scaling in the digital paradigm is non-linear because once a use case is validated, it can be delivered to additional users at near-zero marginal cost. Learning from 10,000 users improves the product for 10 million users at no additional experimental cost. This is why digital businesses can achieve growth rates that industrial businesses cannot.

The Platform Paradigm: The Completed Interaction Is the Engine

The platform paradigm introduces a constraint that neither industrial nor digital organizations typically face: coordinating independent participants whose incentives are only partially aligned, without fully controlling what they produce or do.

Industrial firms create value by transforming inputs into outputs. Digital firms create value by discovering and serving users' needs. Platform firms create value by enabling independent participants to find one another and transact, and by maintaining the conditions that keep those transactions reliable.

The engine of value is the completed interaction: the special moment at which a buyer and seller connect, a host and guest match, a driver and rider are paired, a lender and borrower are introduced, etc. Everything the platform builds—like matching algorithms, trust infrastructure, pricing mechanisms, governance rules, and reputation systems—exists to increase the rate, quality, and reliability of that atomic event.

The binding constraint in the platform paradigm is liquidity under trust. Liquidity is the probability that a participant can find a suitable counterpart at the moment of need. Trust is the confidence that, once initiated, the interaction will proceed reliably. Neither property is valuable without the other: liquidity without trust produces fraud, spam, and eventual collapse; trust without liquidity produces a reliable system that nobody uses because it can't provide what participants need when they need it.

The Hanseatic League fairs of medieval northern Europe understood this centuries before the internet. They developed the medieval infrastructure that enabled high-volume transactions between strangers, using standardized weights, measures, coinage, and enforcement mechanisms.

The platform paradigm's primary goal is to maximize the rate, value, and quality of completed interactions across the participant network. Growth in user count is not the metric that matters. A marketplace with thousands of sellers and insufficient buyers, or with buyers who can't trust sellers to deliver, is failing despite growth in the number of participants. The binding question is always: are participants completing high-quality interactions when they need to, and are the conditions for those interactions improving or degrading over time?

The platform paradigm's feedback loops are network effects. Each additional high-quality participant on one side of the marketplace increases the value of the platform for participants on the other side, attracting more participants and further increasing their value. Unlike industrial-scale (linear with capacity) or digital-scale (non-linear with data), platform-scale compounds are achieved through network density. But it also collapses non-linearly: below a critical threshold of liquidity and trust, the system fails rapidly and discontinuously.

THE THREE PARADIGMS

	INDUSTRIAL	DIGITAL	PLATFORM
Binding Constraint	Throughput At Bottleneck	Speed Of Validated Learning	Liquidity X Trust Threshold
Engine Of Value	Repeatable Process	Validated Use Case	Completed Interaction
Data Role	Control (Stabilize Process)	Learning (Reduce Uncertainty)	Coordination (Enable Matching)
Variation	Cost → Eliminate It	Signal → Exploit It	Consequence → Govern It
Scaling Logic	Linear With Capacity	Horizontal Replication	Super Linear Network Effects
Control Mode Needed	Regulation + Orchestration	Orchestration + Governance	Coordination + Governance

Why the Three Paradigms Cannot be Naïvely Combined

Here is a common system anti-gambit: these three paradigms are not complementary modes that a sufficiently sophisticated business can operate naïvely and simultaneously across the entire organization. Their value engines are misaligned, and their core logic is structurally in direct conflict. Pursuing the goal of one paradigm, with the requisite management discipline to achieve it, actively destroys the conditions needed to achieve the goals of the other two paradigms.

The industrial paradigm demands the elimination of variance: tight process control, predictable output, and low tolerance for deviation. The management discipline that produces manufacturing excellence is precisely the discipline that kills the exploration required by the digital paradigm. A factory manager who has spent a career eliminating variance from production processes will, when asked to build and scale a digital product, instinctively tighten and regulate the process, rather than define a clear use case and open it to variation, experimentation, and validated learning.

The factory manager is not being irrational. They are, in fact, faithfully applying the correct and coherent industrial logic they are familiar with to the new digital-paradigm product they have been tasked with. That's the core conflict of management logic in action.

The result is an organization that demands certainty before shipping, suppresses the variation that would generate learning, and scales before it has validated what it's building. This is definitely not a failure of intelligence; it is instead the structural consequence of applying the right management logic to the wrong paradigm. This is a common system anti-gambit of goal displacement and paradigm change, which, when you look carefully, you will see everywhere.

The digital paradigm demands exploration of variance: rapid iteration, a willingness to be wrong, and a high tolerance for failed experiments. The management discipline that produces learning velocity through short release cycles, reversible decisions, and behavioural instrumentation is precisely the one that destroys the process stability required by the industrial paradigm. "Move fast and break things" in the industrial paradigm will actually end up killing people.

A digital product manager who has built a career on rapid experimentation will, when asked to manage a manufacturing line, introduce variation into processes that require tight control. Cycle times will increase, quality will degrade, and the bottleneck will be unknown rather than clearly identified and controlled. Again, this is not irrationality or incompetence; it is just consistent digital paradigm logic misapplied to an industrial setting.

The platform paradigm demands governance over participants it does not control: trust, infrastructure, consistent rule enforcement, and incentive alignment across independent agents with competing interests. The management discipline that produces platform success through governance frameworks, participant protection, and the willingness to remove bad actors, even at a short-term cost to volume, is incompatible with the throughput-optimization logic of the industrial paradigm and at odds with the speed-of-learning logic of the digital paradigm.

A platform that tries to maximize interaction volume, as an industrial operation maximizes throughput, will rapidly sacrifice trust for scale. A platform that experiments with its governance rules, the way a digital product experiments with features will destroy the predictability and trust that participants need to transact with confidence.

Donella Meadows, whose work on system leverage points remains the most insightful map of where interventions actually matter, identified the goal of a system as one of its highest leverage points. Change the goal, and everything downstream changes with it: the metrics, the management logic, the resource allocation, the definition of success. The three paradigms have distinct goals, binding constraints, engines of value, and compounding feedback architectures.

An organization that tries to run all three without making clear, explicit choices about which logic governs which activity will find that the management logics collide disastrously, and the collisions will systematically generate the worst outcomes of each paradigm rather than the best. That's the ultimate system anti-gambit of goal displacement and paradigm change.

Why “Digital Transformation” Is a Structural Contradiction

Almost all “digital transformation” initiatives fail. The failure rate documented across major consulting firm surveys and business school meta-studies lands at around 87.5%. This number is then typically cited as evidence of poor execution: better change management is needed, greater leadership commitment is required, and clearer roadmaps are essential.

The logical explanation is, in fact, structural: most "digital transformation" initiatives are not a paradigm change. It is the deployment of digital tools within the logic of an industrial paradigm. This increases industrial costs through expensive digital tools, while simultaneously structurally capping the returns of the value that can be created in the digital paradigm, thereby destroying any potential for compounding.

Here is what this looks like in practice. An industrial organization, for example, a manufacturer, a logistics company, or a traditional retailer, decides to "go digital". It deploys machine learning models to optimize its production schedule. It adds predictive maintenance algorithms to its equipment. It builds real-time dashboards that track operational KPIs faster than before.

All of these interventions are marginal improvements. None of them changes the paradigm. The binding constraint is still throughput at the bottleneck. The engine of value is still the repeatable process. The feedback loops are still stabilizing. The management logic is still variance elimination. Digital technology has been added to the industrial paradigm as a better set of tools for what it was already trying to do. The returns are real, but they are also linear and asymptotic: bounded by the same physical constraints they were always bounded by, now approached somewhat more efficiently.

The compounding properties of digital technology, the validated use case, the accelerating learning cycle, and the near-zero marginal cost of replication do not get leveraged in this configuration. They only get leveraged in the digital paradigm, which has a different binding constraint, a different engine of value, and a different management logic.

You cannot access the digital paradigm's compounding returns by adding digital tools to an industrial operation. You have to make the paradigm shift: abandon the goal of throughput optimization in favour of building a structural position based on validated use-case learning and accumulation. That abandonment is the sacrifice. And it looks, from within the industrial paradigm's measurement frame, exactly what it is: a deterioration in current performance on the metrics that matter. Otherwise, it wouldn't be a true sacrifice, and the system gambit requires one.

General Electric's Predix initiative, launched in 2015, is the clearest evidence of this failure at scale. GE invested billions in a platform designed to collect data from industrial equipment, apply machine learning to it, and generate insights that would improve operational performance. The failure of the initiative had nothing to do with the capabilities of digital technology. Instead it failed miserably, because it imported digital paradigm logic into an industrial paradigm context.

GE's industrial customers did not need faster learning cycles about their equipment performance. They needed better control at the bottleneck. They needed feedback mechanisms that prevented deviation, not dashboards that visualized historical trends. GE leadership treated data as a general-purpose asset that could generate value across contexts, but in the industrial paradigm, data serves control rather than learning. The engine of value is the process, not the use case. The feedback loop that matters is stabilizing, not exploratory. Importing digital logic into that structure generated complexity without compounding leverage and produced a write-down of at least $4 billion, according to some sources, and more than $7 billion, according to others.

The lesson for industrial organizations is not to avoid digital technology but instead to operate within the logic of the digital paradigm, whose compounding properties entail different goals, constraints, and management architectures from those of the industrial paradigm. The Tanegashima gun's compounding properties required operating within a military system organized around mass coordination rather than individual valour. You could not access those properties by adopting the use of guns in a samurai army. You had to build an entirely different kind of army.

The Airlines as Proof

The commercial airline industry is one of the most instructive examples available of all three paradigms operating within the same business, and of what happens when an organization deploys the right technology without muddying the value-creation paradigms.

An airline's traditional industrial layer is the physical operations: aircraft, gates, crews, maintenance schedules, turnaround times, fuel consumption, and the tightly coupled chain of processes that converts these inputs into safely completed flights.

The engine of value at this layer is the repeatable process: the standardized operating procedure that reliably moves an aircraft from gate to gate on schedule and at a predictable cost. The binding constraints are throughput at the operational bottleneck: airport slots, aircraft utilization rates, fuel prices, and crew availability. The management logic is industrial: minimize variance, maximize utilization, optimize flow through the constraint.

This is where most airline strategies spent most of the twentieth century. Fleet scheduling software, gate assignment optimization, fine-tuned crew rostering algorithms. All of these are digital tools deployed within the industrial paradigm. The returns did materialize: gate turnaround times and on-time arrivals have improved, and fuel consumption has been optimized. But the returns, despite materializing, were linear and asymptotically flat: bounded by the physics of how fast an aircraft can be turned around, how many airport slots exist, and how many hours a crew can legally fly. No algorithm, however sophisticated, can make an aircraft fly orders of magnitude faster or generate an airport slot that doesn't exist. Digital technology applied to an airline's industrial layer improves industrial operations. It does not change the paradigm.

The first airline to discover the digital paradigm in its business did so not in the maintenance bay or the scheduling office, but in the revenue management function. The question was simple, but the implications were enormous: what if each seat were treated not as an operational output to be utilized, but as an asset whose value could be dynamically discovered and whose price could be maximized through real-time behavioural and demand data?

Dynamic pricing, branded fares, and overbooking changed what the airline was optimizing as its overarching goal. The industrial paradigm asked: what is the minimum cost to operate this aircraft? The digital paradigm asked: what is the maximum revenue this specific seat on this specific flight can generate from this specific customer, given everything we know about their booking behaviour, price sensitivity, alternatives, and timing?

The constraint was no longer operational capacity. There was uncertainty about willingness to pay, and that uncertainty could be systematically reduced through data and algorithms. Every booking confirmed or refuted a pricing hypothesis. Every no-show revealed something about demand elasticity. Every upgrade, whether accepted or declined, sharpened the model for the next iteration.

The optimizing feedback loops needed to change their character. The industrial operation's stabilizing loops, which detect deviations from process standards and correct them, gave way to the digital system's accelerating feedback loops. Each pricing decision generated behavioural data that improved subsequent decisions, which in turn generated better data, thereby refining the model. The marginal cost of adding one more data point to the model was essentially zero.

This goes beyond an incremental improvement on the industrial layer; it represents a different engine of value, operating under different constraints and an entirely different feedback architecture. The airline that confused these two layers, that tried to apply dynamic pricing logic to fleet scheduling, or that tried to apply industrial process discipline to its revenue management experiments, got the worst of both worlds and paradigms: operationally unstable and analytically stagnant.

Picture two identical airlines with the same fleet and the same number of aircraft. Both initially optimize within the industrial paradigm and achieve linear returns that eventually approach an asymptote. Then one airline starts optimizing in the digital paradigm and unlocks an entirely new system of compounding returns. That's the system gambit in action.

The third layer of compounding value emerged from an observation that neither operational efficiency nor revenue optimization could have generated: the most valuable asset an airline had accumulated was not just its routes, gates, fleet, or even its brand. It was its database of verified customer interactions. Every flight taken, every upgrade purchased, every point earned and redeemed was a data point in a rich and priceless behavioural history that could not be rapidly reconstructed by a new entrant, irrespective of the capital deployed. You cannot buy the trust, relationship, and 10 years of shared history. You can only deliberately build, accumulate, and compound it.

Loyalty programmes, seen through this lens, are not marketing expenses as traditionally categorized. They are effectively the airline's platform layer, where loyalty points are network tokens that increase trust and liquidity across an expanding ecosystem of diverse interactions, instead of being liabilities on the balance sheet.

An airline's loyalty programme connects the airline's customers with hotels, car rental companies, credit card issuers, retail partners, and, eventually, any business willing to pay for access to a customer whose behavioural profile the airline has built over years of verified interactions and transactions. Each additional partner expands the network of contexts in which a customer can earn or redeem points, increasing the value of holding miles, the frequency of loyalty-motivated bookings, and the richness of behavioural data, thereby making the loyalty ecosystem more valuable to partners. The engine of value is no longer the seat or the pricing model. It is the completed interaction within the loyalty network: the moment when a behavioural data point is added to a history that no competitor can replicate. That is a structural proprietary advantage that compounds in a unique way by design.

American Airlines' AAdvantage programme, one of the first modern frequent flyer programmes, launched in 1981 as a tactical response to deregulation. By the 1990s, it was generating about the same profit as the airline's flight operations. The platform layer had become more valuable than the industrial layer it was ostensibly designed to support. This is what platform compounding looks like when it runs long enough: the interaction history accumulates, the ecosystem expands, the switching costs deepen, and the gap between the incumbent and any new entrant grows not because the incumbent works harder, but because the loop generates its own super linear growth.

The structural lesson the airline industry teaches is that operating across all three paradigms simultaneously is not necessarily the goal. Rather, each paradigm demands its own management logic, goals, engine of value creation, benchmarks, and definition of success. Importing the logic of one into the operational domain of another caps returns before the compounding can even begin.

An airline that tries to apply industrial variance elimination to its loyalty programme will kill the targeted and dynamic partnerships that keep the platform evolving. An airline that tries to apply digital speed-of-learning logic to its physical operations will introduce the variation that degrades process stability and flight safety. And an airline that tries to build platform interaction density by sacrificing the industrial reliability that makes its flights predictable will destroy the trust that makes its loyalty program valuable in the first place.

Each layer requires its own management logic and discipline. The leadership challenge is to avoid the system anti-gambit of naïvely combining the paradigms. Keeping them distinct while letting them reinforce each other where their interfaces are well designed is the only thing that compounds.

This is exactly what Oda Nobunaga intuitively understood in 1575 and what most organizations still get wrong today. He did not try to adopt guns in the samurai paradigm and make it work. He built a new system organized around the gun's unique asymmetric properties, used his existing yaribusuma formations to cover the gun's structural weaknesses, and let the two systems reinforce each other at their interface while remaining distinct in their organizing logic. The discipline of close-quarters formation combat still governed the spear wall. At the same time, the gunner units were governed by the discipline of coordinated mass fire. He did not ask the gunners to think like samurai. He did not ask the traditional samurai to fight like gunners. He designed the interface between them so that each reinforced the other's strengths without being contaminated or corrupted by the other's management logic.

The organizations that build enduring compounding advantage do the same thing. They are explicitly clear about which paradigm governs which activity. They protect the management logic of each layer from contamination by the others. And they make the sacrifice the paradigm transition requires, abandoning the old paradigm's goal, rather than trying to access the new paradigm's compounding returns while continuing to measure success by the old paradigm's benchmarks. That last move is the structural contradiction at the heart of most "digital transformation". Not poor execution, not insufficient commitment, but a fundamental structural category error about which system the new technology actually belongs to.

> ***The organization most likely to miss the paradigm shift is the one that invested most heavily in measuring the success of the current one.***
>
> ***Your benchmarks are not neutral instruments. They are precision-calibrated to detect the constraint that made you successful in the current system, which is exactly why they cannot detect the new constraint that will make you obsolete in the new system.***
>
> ***Naïve tool adoption brings a new technology to an old question.***
>
> ***The system gambit recognizes that the benchmarks themselves are what need to be sacrificed, and changes them before the market catches up.***

The Second Order Effect

Here is what gets omitted from the Sengoku-era Nobunaga story when it's told as a straightforward triumph of innovation over tradition. Tokugawa Ieyasu was Nobunaga's foremost daimyo ally and general. He fought alongside Nobunaga at Nagashino, absorbed Nobunaga's maverick panache, and, at Sekigahara in 1600, finally ended the civil war and consolidated a unified Japan. Tokugawa Ieyasu was the ultimate survivor of the Sengoku period. He consolidated power, became Shogun, and, in 1600, founded the Tokugawa Shogunate, which would go on to rule Japan for more than 250 years.

Right after becoming Shogun, Ieyasu ruthlessly implemented disarmament and policies that deliberately restricted Japanese firearms development. Production was brought under strict central control, and technical evolution was constrained. The firearm designs that featured at Sekigahara in 1600 remained essentially unchanged throughout the Tokugawa Shogunate, even as European firearms evolved through multiple generations of innovation over the same two and a half centuries.

When Commodore Perry arrived in 1853 with American warships, the technological gap existed not because Japan lacked manufacturing capability or innovative genius. Japan had demonstrated in the late sixteenth century that it could standardize, mass-produce, and deploy firearms on a scale that enabled it to wield more than half of all the world's guns. The gap existed because Tokugawa Ieyasu and the shogunate he founded had intentionally frozen the paradigm for 250 years.

Ieyasu understood something that only a century of brutal civil war can drive home. The same paradigm shift that enabled his master, Oda Nobunaga, to achieve a phenomenal rise and also enabled a peasant like Toyotomi Hideyoshi to become the ruler of unified Japan could enable future challengers to his Shogunate.

If firearms kept evolving, if the paradigm kept shifting, new challengers would keep emerging. The solution was to freeze the paradigm at the point where it had resulted in Tokugawa dominance. Win first, then make it impossible for anyone else to win.

This is the second-order consequence that the system gambit goal displacement and paradigm change can produce: executing the gambit successfully installs a new paradigm, and the organization that built its advantage in the new paradigm immediately acquires the strongest possible incentive to prevent the next paradigm shift.

The new paradigm's winners run the same playbook as the old paradigm's winners. They optimize for the constraint they mastered. They build performance management systems calibrated to the benchmarks of the current paradigm. Those systems are well designed for what they measure. They are structurally blind to the next constraint shift, precisely because their sophistication is organized around the current one.

The airline loyalty programme demonstrates this at scale. The incumbent carriers that have built decades of interaction history and expanded their partner ecosystems have platform advantages that new entrants cannot genuinely replicate. But the depth of that interaction history also creates structural conservatism: the airlines cannot easily change the verification standards and redemption terms on which their trust has been built, because any loosening would erode the asset they've accumulated and invite strong pushback from customers.

When new payment technologies and digital wallet ecosystems began offering alternative loyalty structures with more flexible redemption options and lower friction, the incumbent carriers' measurement systems, optimized to assess the health of the existing loyalty paradigm, were slow to detect the signal. The platform moat and the platform blindness are the same property, viewed from different angles.

This doesn't invalidate the system gambit. It means the three-question test: is the sacrifice real, is the structural condition clear, does the compounding logic actually accelerate, must run continuously, including against the structural position you are currently building. And especially after you succeed in building it.

The system gambit investor–operator who forgets this eventually becomes the Tokugawa Shogunate: the one who wins the paradigm change perfectly, then spends the rest of their tenure ensuring nobody else can execute the same move against them. For more than 250 years, that strategy worked. Then Commodore Perry arrived, and the paradigm that had been frozen in place for a quarter of a millennium collapsed within a few years.

Think, Share, Discuss

Four and a half centuries after the Battle of Nagashino, most boardrooms are still running the defunct daimyo playbook. They evaluate new technology by asking whether it outperforms the old technology on its own benchmarks; it rarely does.

And so the discussion moves to pilot projects, adoption rates, timelines, and ROI models, all built on the assumption that the current constraint remains the decisive one. Basically sophisticated shiny management instruments, pointed at the wrong target, generating confident readings that mean nothing.

This is the system anti-gambit in its purest form: nobody is being irrational, the benchmarks are accurate, but the constraint they're measuring basically stopped mattering to compounding outcomes.

> ***The question that saves the room is not "should we adopt this new technology tool?"***
>
> ***It is: "Which constraint does this shift, and are our benchmarks designed to detect that shift, or to measure the constraint it's replacing?"***

> ***There is a second question immediately after it, and this is the one that reveals whether a genuine system gambit is available: "What would we have to stop measuring, and stop being rewarded for, to build structural position around the new constraint?"***

That second question is where the meeting room usually goes completely silent. Because the answer is always something currently valued, currently visible, and currently on someone's performance review target. That is the sacrifice in its truest form.

The organizations that can identify it, name it, accept it, and build through it are the ones that compound. The ones that don't stay in the vague, meaningless ROI-tweaking company politics: optimizing the metrics of the past with increasing rigour, building moats around positions the next paradigm will render irrelevant.

Nobunaga didn't have more resources than the daimyo he defeated: in fact, he had a tiny province, a lower budget, a small army, and no natural claim to victory. The important lesson is that he won structurally, not just tactically, because he asked the right question early enough and then built a system around the unique asymmetric advantages of the new technology.

The difference was never purely analytical; instead, it was the willingness to make the sacrifice, be publicly ridiculed for it, and keep building while every benchmark in the current paradigm failed to detect his gains. By the time the benchmarks changed, the loop had been running for years. That is the system gambit of goal displacement and paradigm change: not the structural insight but the willingness to sacrifice publicly for it.

You can now identify the mechanism of goal displacement and paradigm change: the binding constraint moves, the old benchmarks go blind to the new source of value, and the first mover who builds a structural position around the new constraint compounds. At the same time, competitors optimize their way towards a carefully measured irrelevance.

SHARE THIS WITH SOMEONE?

Something I finally have language for after years of watching technology investments disappoint:

Most organizations aren't failing at adoption. They're succeeding at it, and yet getting nothing durable in return.

Because they're deploying new tools against old benchmarks, optimizing for constraints that the technology has already made irrelevant.

Oda Nobunaga didn't win because he adopted the gun faster than rival warlords. He won because he recognized the gun belonged to a different paradigm, one that measured success in continuous coordinated concentrated mass firepower rather than individual martial excellence, and was willing to abandon the dominant criterion of the current paradigm to build structural position in the next one.

GE spent billions on Predix trying to make industrial customers learn faster. Industrial customers didn't need to learn faster. They needed better control at the bottleneck: the technology worked but the paradigm logic was wrong.

The companies that build compounding advantage with AI won't be the fastest adopters. They'll be the ones that correctly identified which constraint AI actually shifts, were willing to sacrifice visible performance on the old metrics during the building period, and built structural positions before the paradigm shift became obvious enough for everyone else to see it.

But knowing the constraint has moved is only useful if you can read the signal that tells you where it has moved, and most organizations are not starved of data; they are literally drowning in their data lakes. This is an entirely different anti-gambit system, one that more dashboards and more AI models make worse, not better. The question the next chapter answers is this: what would you have to stop measuring to see the signal that actually governs where the bottleneck is?

GAMBIT TWO

SIGNAL QUALITY: CORE BOTTLENECK

Signal Quality: Core Bottleneck

The candle had almost completely burnt out, its flickering flame casting long shadows across the wood-panelled walls of his study, but Samuel Pepys remained anchored to his desk. It was 2 a.m. on 21 January 1665, a quiet hour when even the bustling London docks were silent, yet his mind raced with the excitement and energy of a man who had just encountered a new hidden world.

Since first seeing the volume at his bookseller's shop on 2 January, he had been eager to own it. Now, with his own copy finally spread open across his desk, the British politician and high-ranking naval administrator found himself utterly captivated. For a while, he completely forgot his maritime concerns. The only thing he could think about was Robert Hooke's *Micrographia*.

Each turn of the heavy page pulled him deeper into a reality that seemed to exist just below the surface of human sight. He leaned forward, his eyes tracing the complexity of a flea's armoured leg and the detailed structures of a louse. These were not simply sketches of insects; instead, they were what he described in his diary as "the most ingenious" observations he had ever read, rendering the mundane into something monumental. When he reached the repetitive structures of cork—what Hooke called "cells", tiny compartments that looked to him like the rooms of monks—Pepys instantly felt religious fervour; he was convinced he had encountered a new way of understanding God's creation.

Three hundred kilometres away in Delft, Antonie van Leeuwenhoek had arrived at a similar instrument by a surprisingly different route. He did not begin as a scholar. He was a linen draper who wanted a better way to inspect the quality of his thread. Driven by a relentless, almost obsessive curiosity through the 1670s, he developed a method for grinding tiny, high-magnification lenses that far surpassed the compound microscopes of his day. Unlike the large, ornate instruments used by Hooke, Leeuwenhoek's devices were handheld silver or brass plates with a single glass bead. When he first peered through them at a drop of stagnant rainwater, he saw what he called "animalcules": countless microscopic creatures swimming with purposeful and autonomous motion.

The revelation of this invisible world struck the seventeenth-century social imagination like a thunderbolt. Before Hooke and Leeuwenhoek, the limits of reality were generally defined by what the naked human eye could see. Now, their work introduced a genuinely unsettling idea: that every surface, the water people drank, the skin on their hands, even the plaque on their teeth, was teeming with life. Public sentiment was a mix of profound awe and deep existential unease, much like the feeling that surrounds AI today. If thousands of "little eels" could inhabit a single drop of water, the human scale of importance suddenly felt less important.

The microscope rapidly became a symbol of a new kind of truth, one that bypassed traditional philosophy and went straight to the raw, unfiltered reality of nature. Heads of state and curious travellers began making detours to Delft to catch a glimpse through Leeuwenhoek's miraculous lenses. By the early 1700s, the microscope had become a status symbol among the wealthy, and a cottage industry of hobbyists had sprung up around it. The tool reshaped behaviour before anyone consciously realized what was going on. Work reorganized around what the instrument made visible.

> ***When outputs arrive faster than understanding, and when a field mistakes new visibility for new understanding, it drifts: not just through incompetence or dishonesty as is commonly framed, but because the instrument pulls practitioners towards what it makes easy rather than what the field can reliably explain.***
>
> ***No one was lying or cutting corners. The tool was doing exactly what it was designed to do. And that was precisely the problem.***

How the Microscope Misled: 150 Years of Hallucinations

It is tempting to see the microscope's early history as a triumph: a new tech tool that opened a hidden world, launched modern biology, and set clinical medicine on the path towards germ theory. That reading is vaguely true. The microscope did reveal something real. Leeuwenhoek's protozoa did exist. Dutch biologist Jan Swammerdam's work on insect anatomy held up under later scrutiny. These were valid discoveries. But if the microscope were, in fact, a revolutionary technological tool, it would have rapidly led to life-changing progress in clinical biology. It didn't for at least 150 years.

Here is what the triumphalist account misses: Hooke never saw living cells, because cork is just dead plant tissue. The regularity he depicted, the clean, ordered compartments that captivated Pepys, did not exist in life as he drew it.

> ***Visibility alone, without any framework capable of interpreting what was being seen, had seduced an entire field into building on an illusion.***

Optically, the microscope was not a failure. The problem was that the tech tool arrived before scientific theories capable of evaluating its outputs had been developed. Techniques like thin-sectioning and staining did not appear until the early 1800s. Köhler illumination was not standardized until 1893. Without standardized procedures or agreed-upon ways for preparing, illuminating, or interpreting tissue, the microscope was a spotlight without a stage. Chromatic aberrations introduced phantom colours. Spherical distortions reshaped smooth surfaces into artificial ridges.

Much of what was recorded as biological structure was, in fact, an artefact of glass and light, irrelevant to the object under study. Two observers could examine the same tissue and disagree entirely about what they saw. Natural philosophers in the eighteenth century documented shapes that vanished under better lenses, organisms that turned out to be bubbles or dust, structures caused by refraction rather than biology. Entire research programmes were built on hallucinations generated by inadequate rigour and faulty process.

This problem persisted for almost 200 years. The instrument increased visibility, but it did not increase understanding. And because the impressions it generated looked detailed, they were easily mistaken for the truth. When different observers reported coherent yet incompatible structures, the very appearance of structure became dangerously misleading. Coherence was mistaken for reality. The human mind naturally assumes that if something looks organized and internally consistent, it must reflect an underlying truth rather than an artefact of the instrument that generated it.

When a field lacks shared criteria for evaluating results, disagreement with prevailing excitement is perceived as incompetence or bad faith rather than as rigorous clarity. Over time, this erodes collective reasoning. People stop arguing about what is true and start arguing about whom to trust, whose output feels right, and which product demo looks most impressive. The field settles questions by reference to who has raised the most money or captured headlines for the longest period. When you question an AI investment and colleagues respond with "but OpenAI raised 6 billion dollars" or "McKinsey says this is transformative", they are not providing evidence or rigorous arguments. Instead they are reverting to the age old trick when no evidence exists: appealing to reputation.

In That Meeting

You have been in that meeting about the AI deployment. The dashboard is open and shared on the screen with everyone: prediction accuracy is glowing green at 83%. There is a silent consensus in the room that the AI initiative is working. That the investment is justified, and that the next phase should proceed. The head of AI adoption is beaming proudly. The AI vendor and the consultant have a cocky grin on their faces.

And yet something nags you, but you're unable to articulate it clearly. The core constraint that caused the most trouble six months ago is still causing trouble, but the dashboard does not show it. It shows the system average instead. You are being asked to approve the next phase of investment, and you have no vocabulary to articulate what feels wrong. So under peer pressure, you approve it along with everyone else.

What you detected was real. The system was performing on the aggregated metrics being tracked. But the loop at the constraint was open, gaping wide. Those are clearly not the same thing, and the dashboard cannot show you the difference because it was never built to close the loop; it was built to aggregate after the loop had already opened or closed elsewhere.

The same mechanism that drove eighteenth-century natural philosophers to build research programmes on optical artefacts is at work in every meeting where an AI's aggregate accuracy is presented as evidence that the right constraint is being measured. The microscope generated visibility then, and the dashboard generates visibility now. Neither one automatically generates compounding knowledge.

SACRIFICE	STRUCTURAL CONDITION	COMPOUNDING LOGIC
Broad monitoring: distributing signal collection evenly across the system at moderate precision. This management logic treats all parts of the system as equally important information sources.	A feedback loop closed at the binding constraint at the granularity decisions require. Signal enters the decision that determines constraint performance; improved performance reveals finer constraint variation; that variation enters the next decision.	Each cycle resolves a simpler constraint problem, revealing the next-level constraint. The loop self-refines: precision compounds without proportional investment increase. Competitors monitoring broadly cannot close this loop from within their architecture.

The Bastogne Bottleneck: Signal Quality at the Bulge

The lesson the history of the microscope proves, and the one that most organizations often miss, is between signal volume and signal placement. These are not variations on the same thing. Signal volume is the quantity of data an organization collects, the number of models it runs, and the number of dashboards it maintains. Signal placement is where in the system those signals close their feedback loop.

A signal placed at the wrong layer of the system, upstream of the bottleneck, downstream of the decision, or aggregated across processes operating at different clock speeds can be perfectly accurate yet completely useless for improving decision-making. The accuracy of the measurement and the relevance of its placement are independent properties. Confusing them is what early adopters of the microscope did. It is what most AI deployments do today.

In December 1944, Hitler's Nazi army launched Operation Watch on the Rhine: an offensive with around 400,000 men of three armies designed to break the Allied lines through the frozen dense Ardennes forest. To move 1,400 tanks through the Ardennes forest, the Nazis needed paved roads. In the craggy, forested terrain of the Belgian panhandle, those roads converged at one place: Bastogne. General Anthony McAuliffe hunkered down in Bastogne, with a few thousand troops and only a few dozen remaining tanks to face a Nazi enemy that had surrounded him.

The sacrifice McAuliffe made was informational. In the chaos of the Ardennes, most Allied units were drowning in noise: conflicting reports, severed communication lines, and the horrifying panic of a perimeter that seemed to be collapsing simultaneously from every direction.

McAuliffe sacrificed broad situational coverage. He held the hub with everything he had. Because his world was smaller and his position was central, his information moved faster and with less distortion than the enemy's. He gave up the ability to monitor every arc of the battle in exchange for something more valuable: a high-fidelity signal at the exact constraint that determined the outcome of the entire battle.

What he purchased with that sacrifice was a closed feedback loop at the bottleneck: the only thing that mattered. Because the 101st held the hub of a seven-way junction, they could shift resources across the town's diameter in minutes. The Nazis, attacking along the perimeter, had to travel long, exposed arcs to coordinate. Whenever a German probe hit the thin outer screen, McAuliffe could slide reserves across the centre to meet it, because his signal quality was high enough to pinpoint exactly where the pressure was rising before the attackers could coordinate their next move.

Each successful repulse gave his engineers more time to lay mines and his infantry more time to fortify the next sector. Every failed Nazi thrust increased the relative density of the American perimeter while the Nazi offensive dissolved into logistical noise. The loop kept compounding. The defence was a self-reinforcing feedback loop, with each cycle producing conditions that made the next more productive, until, by 23 December, the bottleneck had starved the Nazi spearhead of the momentum it needed to reach the Meuse River. The signal loop closed at the constraint, enabling compounding.

Toyota's development of the kanban system in the 1950s operates on the same structural logic, but translated to industrial production. Using Kanban to generate data for inventory levels is dashboard thinking applied to a pre-dashboard system, misses the point entirely.

Kanban was designed to prevent inventory from accumulating in ways that would mask production problems at the bottleneck. Each card authorized the production or movement of a specific quantity. When cards were exhausted, production stopped. Problems that would have been hidden by buffer inventory became immediately visible because they stopped the line. The data, which was essentially a physical card indicating the presence or absence of authorization, existed to regulate behaviour at the core constraint and to make deviations from the target state impossible to ignore or rationalize away.

The power of this system lay not in the sophistication of the data or tech tools, but in its placement and its speed. The signal was local, at the point where decisions about production and material flow were made. It was binary: either authorization existed, or it did not, eliminating delays in interpretation. Most importantly, it was physical, which made it impossible to dismiss or ignore. And it operated at the clock speed of the actual production process rather than at the tempo of weekly management reports or monthly reviews. Simple, local, and fast is the combination that keeps the loop closed.

Now consider what happens when an organization replaces that system with a comprehensive data platform or a lake house. Sensors are added throughout the facility. Data streams aggregate into a central data lake house. Machine learning models are trained to predict machine performance based on historical patterns. Dashboards are built for management, showing utilization trends, energy efficiency, maintenance history, and quality metrics across shifts and product lines.

If this implementation focuses on aggregation, visualization, and prediction without strengthening the feedback loop at the key bottleneck, it will reduce system performance rather than improve it. The operators who control the constraint now receive their information through generic prebuilt BI dashboards rather than direct feedback at the bottleneck, where signal quality is highest, and so the delay between deviation and correction increases as the clock speed slows.

The models generate predictions that may or may not align with the process's immediate state. Management's attention shifts to KPIs that reflect historical performance and trends, rather than to the current state of the bottleneck and the feedback loop driving it. The system becomes slower to respond, more complex to interpret, and more fragile under stress. The dashboards look fine, but the signal is drifting, and the constraint is not tracked.

This is precisely what happened when GM managers rotated through NUMMI, the pioneering joint venture between Toyota and GM, in the 1980s, as they tried to replicate Toyota's practices at other facilities. They copied the visible elements, like kanban cards, Andon cords, and quality circles, but without understanding the first-principles systems logic that made those practices coherent, as described in the signal quality system gambit.

They implemented stop-line authority without reorganizing workflows to ensure problems could be addressed quickly when production stopped. They reduced inventory buffers without developing the supplier relationships and internal coordination that made low-inventory operation viable. They created quality circles without changing the management systems that determined whether worker suggestions would be acted upon. The practices failed in isolation because they were designed as integrated components of a signal system rather than as standalone tools. The loop required all its components to be present to close, and naïvely copying any subset of them left the loop open.

What the GM failure reveals is that each component of Toyota's system was a high-quality signal device whose function depended on the presence of every other component. Remove any one of them, and you do not just have a degraded version of the system, but you have a system whose signal loop is not closed.

The Andon cord is a constraint-level signal instrument. When a worker pulls it, they are placing a signal at the exact point in the system where a problem has appeared: not upstream, not in a management report one layer above the line, but exactly at the constraint itself, and at the moment the deviation occurs. That placement is the entire point. GM installed the cords and gave workers the authority to pull them, but GM did not reorganize the workflow to receive that signal at constraint clock speed.

When a worker pulled the cord at a Toyota plant, a team leader was at the station within 60 seconds, with the authority and problem-solving framework to address the issue before the line had to stop. When a worker pulled the cord at a GM plant running Toyota's visible rituals, the signal propagated upwards through a management structure designed for a different purpose, one that had never been rebuilt around the assumption that constraint-level signals would arrive continuously and require immediate response. The signal existed. The loop could not close because the receiving infrastructure was never built.

The inventory buffer failure is structurally different but produces the same result. Toyota eliminated buffers specifically because buffers mask constraint-level signals. When a process upstream of the bottleneck produces defective parts and a buffer exists between them, the defects accumulate covertly. The bottleneck keeps running on good parts from the buffer, and the problem is invisible and undetected until the buffer runs out, by which point the upstream process has produced a large quantity of defective work, and the root cause is harder to trace. Toyota understood that the buffer was not protecting the system, instead, it was actually protecting the problem.

Eliminating the buffer forced every constraint-level deviation to propagate immediately, making it impossible to ignore and enabling rapid, on-source resolution. GM eliminated the buffers without developing the supplier relationships and internal coordination that made low-inventory operations viable, so when deviations propagated, there was no framework to distinguish constraint-level signals from downstream noise. Every problem looked equally urgent, and nothing was clearly identifiable. The system produced chaos rather than clarity because the signal architecture required to make constraint-level deviations actionable had never been built.

Quality circles explicitly place signal authority with the workers most proximate to the constraint: basically, the people who can observe, in real time, which specific conditions cause the process to improve or fail. That is the correct placement. The problem is that the loop terminates at the management level. For quality circle feedback to close the loop, the management system must be structured to receive and act on those signals, which requires both authority and incentives.

In Toyota's system, quality circle suggestions fed directly into the continuous improvement process, where team leaders and engineers with genuine authority over process design would investigate, test, and implement changes. In GM's version, suggestions entered a management hierarchy designed around an entirely different logic, one in which production volume was the primary performance metric and line changes were costly, disruptive, and to be avoided. The signal existed, but middle management had neither the authority to act on it nor the incentive to try. The loop opened at the management layer and stayed open there.

The same failure recurs in every data pilot that succeeds in a sandbox but collapses in production. The demand forecasting model, trained on clean historical data, produces plausible predictions under controlled conditions. Then it encounters the real system: production data that arrives late, contains errors, and uses inconsistent definitions across business units.

The model's predictions cannot be integrated into the production planning process because that process was designed around different forecast cadences, aggregation levels, and planning horizons. The planners who would use the forecasts lack the authority to adjust production schedules because manufacturing capacity was allocated months ago. The loop never closes. The model keeps generating predictions. The constraint continues to run on its own logic, unaffected. Nothing really changes.

Adding more data sources does not close this loop. When performance can be segmented across hundreds of variables, the ability to fit historical patterns with impressive precision increases, but if those patterns reflect correlations without a causal mechanism, if they capture relationships that were stable in the training period but will break when conditions change, the additional dimensions create false confidence. The microscope enabled eighteenth-century natural philosophers to make more observations. What they needed was fewer observations, placed at the right point, interpreted by a framework capable of making sense of them.

C. Hoare & Co., founded on Fleet Street in 1672, is the UK's oldest privately owned bank and is still owned today by descendants of its founder. It has existed for more than 350 years.

The core binding constraint in traditional banking is adverse customer selection. For a bank whose partners hold unlimited personal liability, the wrong customer can destroy partners' personal wealth and a reputation built over generations. As Henry Hoare put it, banking is straightforward if you avoid the mad and the bad. Every other metric in the business is downstream of getting this one decision right.

Hoares bank places its highest-fidelity signal quality precisely at this core bottleneck. Every prospective customer is met in person by a partner. The partner makes the admission decision: not a credit committee, not an automated risk model, not a KYC platform. The cycle time is typically twenty-four hours.

The sacrifice is obvious and ongoing: JPMorgan employs more than a thousand data scientists, while Hoares bank employs about half a dozen. Alexander Hoare proudly states that the bank has consistently and knowingly ignored "best practices" in IT management for decades.

When the Regulator imposed Know Your Customer (KYC) requirements in the early 2000s, Hoares bank complied by collecting passports and utility bills and, in its own assessment, identified not a single customer it did not already know. Many customers knew across multiple generations.

Unlimited liability is the architectural feature that makes the system gambit work at Hoares bank. In a limited-liability bank, the aggregation layer is authoritative because no individual has standing to override it. In a partnership where partners' personal wealth is on the line, the partner who meets the customer is operating not at some vague aggregate layer, but directly at the highest-quality signal at the core bottleneck. The aggregation layer cannot override the partner's decision, because the aggregation layer is not the one with capital at risk. This is the same Toyota property GM failed to replicate at NUMMI: the locus of decision cannot be moved upward without dissolving the signal that makes the system work.

The compounding loop runs on a timescale well beyond the chapter's other examples. Many current customer relationships were initiated by the great-grandparents of today's account holders. Each admission cycle, each surviving relationship, and each rare failure add to the partners' tacit model of which conditions predict customer quality. The resolution exceeds anything an aggregation system could match within a single human career.

The result is phenomenal compounding returns. With a £7 billion balance sheet, a handful of data scientists, and an explicit intent to stay relatively small, Hoares bank is, by its senior partner's own assessment, probably the most profitable bank in the country. Three hundred and fifty years of constraint-cycle self-refinement cannot be purchased. It can only be built through rigorous signal quality at the core bottleneck.

> ***Most organizations ask whether their AI is making better predictions. The question that determines whether those predictions compound is very different: does the signal loop close at the binding constraint, or does it terminate at an intermediate layer?***
>
> ***A model with 95% accuracy, trained on aggregated data, several steps removed from the bottleneck, produces precise forecasts of the wrong thing.***
>
> ***The sacrifice is the neat looking always green management dashboard. What it purchases is the only loop that actually accelerates and compounds.***

The Paradox: How AI Adoption Scales the Problem

Here is the paradox that the sophistication of modern AI deployment has genuinely hidden. The organizations with the most advanced data infrastructure, the most data, the most models, and the most dashboards are, ironically, often the most vulnerable to the system anti-gambit described in this chapter. Their measurement systems can accurately track AI tool outputs, including prediction accuracy, average throughput, cost per unit, and model confidence scores.

What those systems cannot track is whether the signal loop at the binding constraint remains closed, because that loop was never instrumented in a way that AI can make sense of. People made a specific judgement about the operator, who has run the digester for 11 years and knows from a particular vibration pattern that the process is about to degrade before any sensor can detect it.

In the team's institutional tacit knowledge of the understanding of which combination of upstream conditions produces constraint tightening three shifts later. When AI systems replace those people, or when dashboards replace their judgment, the loop opens without anyone noticing it. The dashboards look fine because they were never measuring the loop in the first place anyway.

The prettier the dashboard, the more thoroughly the constraint-specific feedback loop can be destroyed without anyone noticing. The paradox is problematic: the better your AI tools perform in the aggregate, the easier it becomes to destroy the high-quality signal loop that makes the aggregate meaningful, and the harder it becomes to detect that this loop is broken, because the KPIs tracking AI performance will not show it. A system in which the constraint loop has been stealthily open for six months can look, from the dashboard layer, indistinguishable from a system in which it is closed.

Think, Share, Discuss

The key question that changes the nature of the conversation in any meeting room where an AI deployment is being reviewed:

> ***"Before we approve this, has anyone identified the core binding constraint, and confirmed that its signal reaches a decision-maker at that constraint rather than terminating at an intermediate layer where the signal gets lost?"***

If the answer is immediately clear: constraint named, placement confirmed, loop closed, then the deployment has been designed correctly. If the answer is hesitation, an appeal to the ML model's accuracy, or a reference to the comprehensiveness of the data behind the dashboard, then you have found the placement gap: the loop is open.

SHARE THIS WITH SOMEONE?

I just understood why our AI investments keep producing useless results in pilots and disappointing in production. The models themselves are not bad; they are bult in the wrong system.

We've been measuring model performance at the aggregate level while the constraint, the actual bottleneck whose behaviour determines system performance, runs on its own logic, unaffected.

The signal loop at the bottleneck was never closed.

Every dashboard we built on top of it made that invisible, because dashboards aggregate after the loop has already opened or closed. If I'd had this frame three years ago, I'd have asked one different question before approving any of the last five data platform investments: where exactly does this signal terminate? Does it reach the constraint, or does it stop at a layer of management visibility above it?

You can now locate the placement gap: where the signal terminates before the constraint, rather than at it. Closing that gap is the necessary move. What remains is a much harder question. A signal at the constraint tells you the digester temperature is drifting, or the packaging line is slowing, or that the bottleneck is likely tightening, but it does not tell you why.

For that, you need something most organizations have stopped caring about in the age of AI and dashboards: a model of the mechanism that converts the signal into a specific, committed prediction about what will happen next if you do not act. That model cannot be built by pattern matching on historical training data alone. AI cannot generate it, and building it requires a sacrifice that most company cultures resist entirely: the willingness to be explicitly and demonstrably wrong.

What would it cost your organization to commit, in advance, to an explanation of why your constraint behaves the way it does: one accurate enough that next week's data could prove it wrong?

GAMBIT THREE

CAUSAL MODEL: EXPLANATORY PRECISION

Causal Model: Explanatory Precision

The candle on the old wooden table has burned to a stub, and the young mathematician sitting beside it has stopped pretending to work. It is October 1601 in Prague, and outside the window, the city moves through its ordinary routine: carts rolling on cobblestones, the distant clang of a church bell, the cold stench of the river, indifferent to what is happening in this room.

In bed, a man with a shiny gold-hued copper alloy nose prosthetic drifts in and out of consciousness, and when consciousness comes, it brings the same Latin phrase, repeated in a kind of delirious insistence, as though saying it enough times might result in an answer from the dark: ne frustra vixisse videar.

Let me not seem to have lived in vain. The man is Tycho Brahe, 54 years old, 11 days into a slow dying that began at a regal banquet where, as etiquette in 1601 demanded of aristocrats, he refused to leave the table to urinate. This significantly damaged his bladder. The young mathematician is Johannes Kepler, and as he sits listening to those words uttered repeatedly in the dark, he finds himself visualizing, almost involuntarily, the life of the man in the bed: a life so improbable, so outsized, so streaked with both grandeur and catastrophe that it feels less like a biography and more like something a novelist or movie director would have been asked to tone down.

He thinks, perhaps, first of the nose. Everyone thinks first of the nose, especially because it is a gleaming golden prosthetic fixed to the face with adhesive paste. On 29 December 1566, a professor hosted an engagement party in Rostock. Lots of wine had been consumed, and two young Danish noblemen spent the better part of three weeks nursing a grievance about which of them was the superior mathematician. In the darkness of that winter evening, they bizarrely chose to resolve it with swords.

When the duel is over, the 20-year-old Tycho Brahe is missing the bridge of his nose, taken cleanly off by his third cousin, Manderup Parsberg. For the remaining 35 years of his life, Brahe wears a prosthetic fixed to his face with an adhesive paste he carries in a small vial wherever he goes. Unfazed by rivals who used the golden nose to ridicule him, Tycho made it part of his larger-than-life aristocratic flamboyance. He and Parsberg eventually became close friends.

What the golden nose symbolizes is more than eccentricity: it is the most apt representation of a man incapable of being stopped by setback, embarrassment, or the judgement of people who have not done what he has done. Kepler also knows the stranger facts, the ones that sit beneath the public legend and that are not widely known.

He knows that Tycho Brahe did not begin life in the house he was born into: when he was roughly two years old, his childless uncle Jørgen took him from his parents' home, and his parents appear to have consented, which seems inexplicable even today. Part of Kepler detests Tycho because the man grew up inside the dense web of Danish nobility. But he also admires the gritty stubbornness that compelled Tycho to spend countless nights measuring the stars with methodical precision.

And then of course there is the island.

By 1576, Tycho Brahe had persuaded the Danish king Frederick II to grant him Hven, a small island in the Øresund Strait, along with a substantial royal stipend. What he built on Hven was much more than a mere astronomical observatory. Uraniborg was the first purpose-built scientific research institution in European history: a main observatory, an underground secondary facility constructed to protect instruments from wind, an alchemical laboratory in the basement, its own printing press, its own paper mill powered by the overflow of a fish pond, and even a small prison at the gatehouse. For 20 years, he made detailed nightly observations of planetary positions, achieving a precision of one arcminute: a tenfold improvement on anything that had existed before him.

He also kept a tame elk, which roamed the grounds and entertained visiting dignitaries. Then one evening, it is rumoured the elk drank loads of beer, climbed the castle stairs, and fell to its death. Brahe even had to write to a colleague who had hoped to receive the animal and explain, with whatever diplomatic resources he could muster, that this was no longer possible. He also kept a dwarf named Jepp, a court jester he weirdly believed to be clairvoyant, about whom troubling rumours circulated.

It matters that all of these absurd-sounding things are simultaneously true. The arcminute precision, the drunken duelling, the metal nose, and the beer-loving elk are not contradictions of the same life: they are rich facets of the same life, expressed with deep intensity and blaring volume à la Tycho Brahe.

Kepler also knows how it ended: the first big ending, well before the eventual and final ending in this room. In 1588, Brahe's longtime patron, King Frederick II, died, and the new king, Christian IV, looked at Brahe's expenses with considerably less warmth, annoyed perhaps by the persistent but unverifiable rumours concerning Tycho and the queen mother. As funding disappeared, Brahe left Denmark in 1597, taking his instruments and his two decades' worth of irreplaceable data to Prague. From there, he wrote to Galileo twice in Padua, proposing a collaboration. Galileo, still a decade away from the fame of the telescope, did not reply to either letter.

Eventually, Kepler had arrived, in the winter of 1600, a Protestant refugee from Austria, the grandson of an innkeeper, essentially as poor as Brahe was wealthy. Their 18 months together were strained in the way that collaborations between men of radically different class and radically different conviction tend to be strained: Brahe releasing data in small controlled batches, Kepler burning to test his theories against real numbers, both of them arguing, both of them working, the friction between them generating more heat than either would have chosen but also more light than either could have produced alone.

The problem Brahe had given Kepler was Mars: the most orbitally eccentric of the visible planets, the most demanding, the one most capable of revealing what was actually true about the structure of the solar system.

Now, sitting in the candlelight with those words reverberating through the room, Kepler understands something about the man in the bed that he perhaps could not have understood 18 months ago: that the fear gnawing at his soul is real, and that it has always been real, running beneath everything. Brahe has spent his entire life building an argument for a certain view of the cosmos, and he does not know whether his painstaking work will make a dent in the astronomical universe. On his deathbed, he makes one final request: that Kepler complete the great astronomical tables they have been compiling, and use the data to prove the Tychonic system true.

What Kepler cannot tell him, because he does not yet know himself, is that the data will prove nothing of the kind. That he will take Brahe's Mars observations and spend years working through calculations that bring him to the edge of abandoning the problem entirely, until he finds that the only curve fitting every single data point is not a circle but an ellipse.

This discovery will dismantle Brahe's model, along with every other model built on circular orbits. That Brahe's 20 years of precision measurement will prove Brahe's own cosmology wrong, and in doing so lay the foundation for Kepler's three laws of planetary motion, and through them eventually Newton's theory of gravity, and thanks to that, ultimately a new mathematical architecture for the entire universe.

For now, Kepler can only sit, and listen, and start to wonder, for the first time, perhaps, with the full gravity of the scene, what those two decades on a Danish island measuring the sky actually cost a man, and what they were worth.

Brahe was wrong to be worried. But he could not have known that. The answer to his prayer was already written in the data he was leaving behind: in measurements so precise that they would outlast his theory, outlast his model of the universe, and outlast everything except the truth he had, without knowing it, already found.

TIMELINE OF KEY EVENTS

1546

1546 — 1601: Life of Tycho Brahe

1572 — 1577: Tycho observes a "new star" (supernova) and a great comet, proving the heavens are not immutable.

1600: Johannes Kepler becomes Tycho's assistant in Prague.

1601: Tycho dies; Kepler gains access to his lifelong data.

1609: Kepler publishes *Astronomia Nova*, containing his first two laws.

1610: Galileo Galilei publishes *Sidereus Nuncius*, detailing his first telescopic discoveries.

1619: Kepler publishes *Harmonice Mundi*, introducing his third law.

1632: Galileo publishes *Dialogue Concerning the Two Chief World Systems*, leading to his trial in 1633.

1632

Measuring Everything and Fearing Futility: Ne Frustra Vixisse Videar

Here is the conventional reading of Brahe's story: a brilliant, vain man spent 20 years building the most comprehensive astronomical dataset in history in service of a cosmological model that proved wrong.

That reading of history gets the lesson completely wrong. Brahe's data did not survive because it was big and comprehensive. Big comprehensive data that can be bent to fit any cosmological model would have been useless to Kepler: just another set of numbe rs that clever enough epicycles could accommodate. What made Brahe's measurements irreplaceable was precisely that they could not be bent. They were so precise, one arcminute, 10 times better than anything before them, that they shattered every model that tried to accommodate them without being true, including Brahe's own.

Kepler's laws were powerful not because they fit the data. Many epicycle models could be fine-tuned to match observed planetary positions with comparable accuracy. They were powerful because they were hard to vary. Change the elliptical orbit to any other shape, and the entire mathematical structure breaks down. Adjust the relationship between orbital period and distance from the sun, and predictions for all other planets immediately fail. The explanation's power came from its internal necessity, from the fact that its components could not be modified arbitrarily without destroying its coherence.

This is what Brahe built without knowing he was building it. It was, sadly, not proof of his preferred cosmology, but rather a dataset so constrained that it could only be explained by the truth. The precision was the system's gambit. The sacrifice was 20 years of obsessive measurement that yielded, in the short run, nothing his theory could use. The structural condition purchased was data that was too hard to vary without breaking. The compounding: that data outlasted every theory that tried to accommodate it and eventually generated the only explanation that fit, one that Brahe, unfortunately, never lived to see.

In That Meeting

The quarterly review runs for two hours. Slides advance, showing regional performance breakdowns, customer segment analyses, conversion funnel metrics, all colour-coded and precise to two decimal places. Someone presents a new machine learning model that predicts churn with 83% accuracy. The CFO nods approvingly while the CMO asks a small technical question about methodology. Then someone asks what happens if you raise prices by 8% in the mid-market segment, and the room goes quiet.

The data person says they could run an analysis in two or three days. The revenue leader says it depends on the competitive response. The product person mentions something vague about value perception in that particular market segment.

All true, all reasonable. But critically, none of it answers the question because nobody in the meeting room can draw a clear path from the proposed change through the actual mechanism by which customers make purchase decisions to a predicted outcome. Despite 127 real-time dashboards tracking every conceivable KPI, no one can answer the question rigorously. The organization can observe everything. But it understands almost nothing.

Admiral Hyman Rickover, who built and ran the US Navy's nuclear submarine programme for 30 years, had a documented approach to selecting officers. Accounts from those who went through his selection process describe a pattern: he would probe a candidate's position, then push back hard, not with new evidence or counterargument, but with authority and displeasure alone. He was looking to see whether the candidate would change their answer.

Most did. Confronted with that kind of pressure, most men began to qualify, hedge, and find previously unnoticed merit in whatever position the admiral seemed to prefer. This is a natural response. It is also, in a submarine with a malfunctioning nuclear reactor at 900 feet, a very lethal one. Rickover didn't care about the confidence of candidates. He was interested in testing whether a person's conclusion was connected to his reasoning or to the mood of the room. Those are two very different things, and they can produce officers of very different calibre.

The deeper point here is about what a model of the world actually is. A real causal model, one that traces how specific inputs produce specific outputs through specific mechanisms, is hard to vary without breaking it. Change one assumption and the conclusions change in predictable ways. That constraint is what makes it useful. A position that shifts under social pressure alone, that bends to accommodate whoever is currently applying pressure, is not a rigorous causal model. As I argued in Data Impact, this is groupthink masquerading as "best practices" to ensure social comfort. What Rickover was selecting for was the officer whose answer had a rock-solid foundation, rigorously grounded in reasoning rather than in the mood or atmosphere of the room. That is the thing that holds when everything else is going wrong.

> ***Business leaders today possess unprecedented volumes of data while simultaneously losing the discipline of constraining explanations through causal mechanism. When data can be segmented across dozens of dimensions, like for example by geography, by vertical, by segment, by channel, and the degrees of freedom available for constructing explanations that fit observed patterns expand dramatically. An explanation that accommodates any outcome by adjusting how the data is sliced provides no constraint on what will happen next. An explanation is useful not when it can be made to fit observations, but when it cannot be modified without breaking.***

That's the gap from that quarterly review. The organization has reporting, analytics, and forecasting capabilities. Still, it lacks the explanatory constraint that makes input measurements tell you what will happen next, rather than just describing what happened in the past.

SACRIFICE	STRUCTURAL CONDITION	COMPOUNDING LOGIC
Explanatory flexibility: the ability to accommodate any observed outcome by adjusting parameters, adding variables, or reframing context. This management logic treats model adjustment as sophisticated analysis.	A hard-to-vary causal model: every component load-bearing, every prediction falsifiable, every failure precisely located. The model fails definitively when wrong, revealing exactly which component failed, enabling targeted revision rather than arbitrary adjustment.	Successful tests extend confident prediction to new domains. Failures precisely locate errors and produce more tightly constrained revisions. Each cycle: model more constrained, predictions more reliable, failures more informative. The loop self-improves towards higher precision, not higher complexity.

The Four Modes of System Control: Regulation, Coordination, Orchestration and Governance

A flexible model, one that can accommodate any observed outcome by adjusting how the data is sliced, cannot be falsified by evidence. Thus, evidence cannot improve it either. And because evidence cannot improve it, each additional data cycle yields no improvement in the model's predictive performance, so there is no compounding of value. After five years of data accumulation, the flexible model inhabits the same explanatory territory it started in. The data has grown, and yet tragically, the understanding has not. The irony is that you can have the best data and AI tech stack and yet not have created any value.

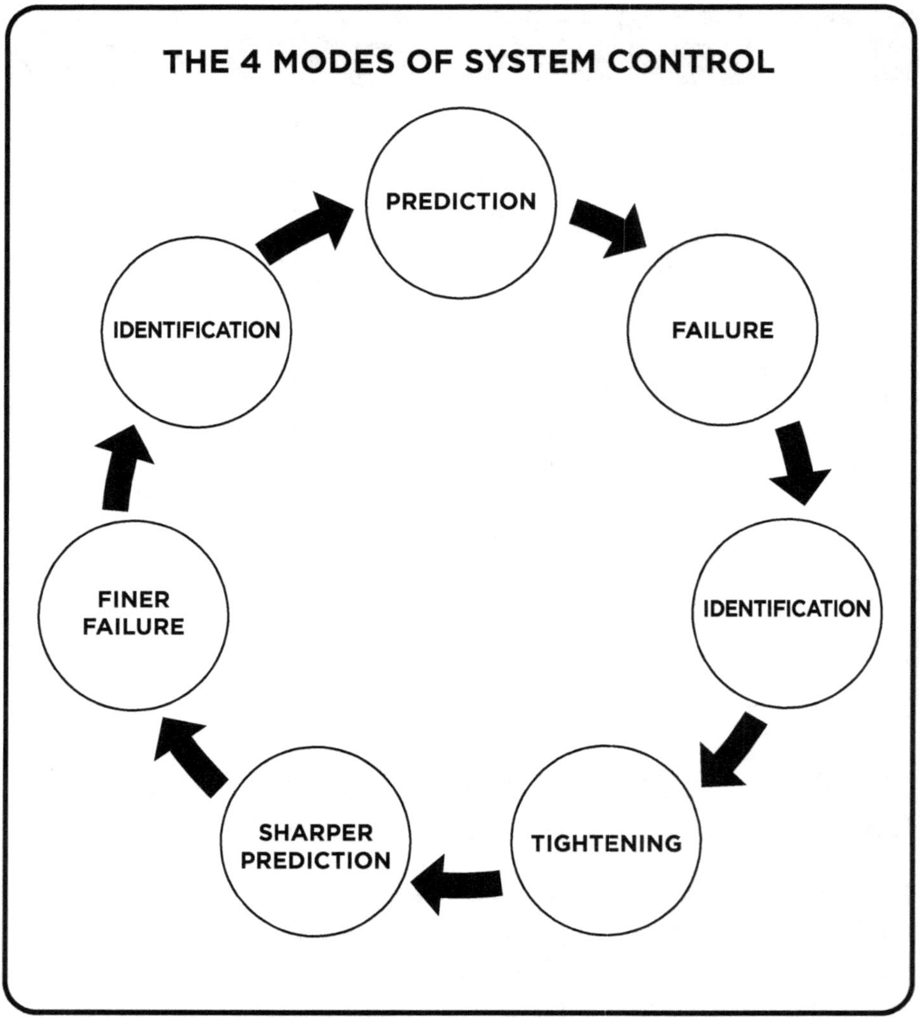

The hard-to-vary model inverts this at every step. Its internal load-bearing logic causes it to break when a prediction fails. Each crack exposes which aspects and elements were wrong. Fixing that element generates better predictions. Better predictions expose finer deviations in the next cycle. Fine-tuning, which addresses deviations, further improves the model, leading to value compounding.

The loop runs: prediction → failure → identification → improvement → better prediction → finer failure → identification.

Each cycle makes the next cycle more informative without requiring a proportional increase in input. After five years, the hard-to-vary model occupies a realm of understanding that the flexible model cannot access: not because it has more data, but because its architecture converts data into constraints rather than achieving wider coverage.

The distinction between these two types of models is not obvious in the short run. In the short run, the flexible model looks more generalizable and more powerful. It fits everything, and vendors and consultants sell you precisely this system anti-gambit. The hard-to-vary model looks incomplete because it breaks. The misplaced competitive pressure in most organizational environments pushes towards the flexible model, because breaking is embarrassing and a vague "cover your ass" generalization is rewarded in corporate politics. This is the system anti-gambit that is evident across most organizations: the rational, locally optimal response to an environment that rewards superficial coverage over explanatory clarity.

What this produces over time is organizations that accumulate years of data without gaining any decisive understanding. The reason for this has a structural explanation, based on the four modes of systems control described below.

Regulation maintains the system state within bounds through continuous feedback: a thermostat detects deviation from the setpoint. It triggers a corrective response without understanding why 20°C matters or what consequences the deviation entails.

Coordination aligns timing between independent agents without controlling what those agents are trying to accomplish: a traffic light sequences who proceed without governing destinations or routes.

Orchestration executes predefined workflows by sequencing dependent activities without deciding what those workflows should accomplish: a conductor keeps time without composing the music, working from an existing score.

None of these three modes requires a causal model. Each can be automated, copied, or licensed. Each can be improved incrementally through more sophisticated tooling. This is precisely why deploying AI to improve regulation, coordination, or orchestration, however impressive the demos, does not generate compounding advantage. You are improving execution within constraints set by someone else's decisions.

Governance is different.

Governance makes binding decisions under uncertainty by arbitrating between competing objectives and accepting accountability for consequences. A ship's captain facing a storm must decide whether to risk damage maintaining schedule, burn extra fuel going around, or seek shelter, accepting delay. That decision requires a causal model of how each choice propagates through the system the captain is operating: what forces the ship can withstand, how the weather will evolve, what contractual obligations exist, and what risks are genuinely acceptable. Without a model of that system, the captain has no basis for arbitrating between trade-offs.

Governance is the only mode of system control that generates compounding advantage. Each governance cycle that makes a specific prediction, observes the outcome, and updates the model is an improvement cycle.

The causal model gets more constrained. The next prediction is better. The next break is more informative. Organizations that confuse orchestration with governance, invest in workflow automation and call it a strategic capability, are investing in a mode of system control that does not compound. They are building a faster, more efficient musical score-reading system in an environment where the competitive advantage lies with whoever is composing the music. These are two completely different systems.

AI can potentially regulate when bounds are predefined. It can coordinate when protocols are explicitly stated. It can even orchestrate workflows with limited efficiency. But it cannot govern, because governance requires a grounded causal model of your particular system, the kind built through years of predictions that broke in various ways and were improved relentlessly. When an organization uses AI to automate governance, it forgoes the structural conditions for compounding and shifts the only compounding form of system control to a tool that cannot execute it.

This is why a hard-to-vary causal model is the very structural foundation of the only mode of system control that generates durable advantage and compounds value. The mechanism by which this plays out is clearest not in failure but in success, for example, in one of the most impressively governed systems in the history of commercial technology.

ASML, the Dutch maker of extreme ultraviolet lithography machines, does not sell products in any conventional sense. Its machines, each priced at $450 million, print the circuit patterns that make modern semiconductors possible, operating at tolerances measured in fractions of a nanometre, where a single vibration from a passing truck can destroy a wafer batch. By ASML's own logic, what it sells is not a machine but a process designed for different use cases: the ability to sustain reliable, high-yield lithography inside a customer's semiconductor fab, continuously, under real production conditions, across years of operation, for different kinds of chips.

When an EUV system underperforms at a particular customer fabrication plant, with degraded yield, unexpected variability, or throughput below specification, essentially all equipment manufacturers treat this as a support problem. Fix the symptom, restore the metric, move on, and pretend nothing happened. ASML treats it as a failed causal prediction. The failure helps identify which element of their causal model of EUV behaviour was wrong: which interaction among the laser, tin droplet, mirror, vacuum, and customer process they had not understood sufficiently well. Every plant, every process node, every operating environment is a live experiment. The causal model improves through variation across instances, which provides the data for learning rather than outliers to be filtered out.

The compounding runs in one direction only: each break in throughput reveals what was wrong, each correction generates a more constrained understanding of how EUV actually behaves in reality for that context, each constrained understanding enables better performance for the next chip-making machine generation, and at a more meta-level, each generation produces failures that improve the model further.

ASML has been running this loop for decades. The understanding embedded in their current EUV machine generation extends beyond having more data than competitors possess. Because, it reflects a causal architecture that has been broken and improved hundreds of thousands of times in real production environments, in ways no competitor has yet experienced or can purchase on the market.

No one can buy 25 years of operating and learning from this loop. No one can license the institutional memory of which specific things failed in which specific fabs, and what those failures revealed about the mechanism. You can only run this loop by first making predictions precise enough to break. That is the sacrifice. That is the structural condition. That is why ASML's position has proven durable over decades, even under extraordinary geopolitical pressure. What constitutes the moat is the explanatory precision built through decades of causal model-building at a global institutional scale.

Now consider what the system anti-gambit looks like at scale: not as a failure of resources or intelligence, but as the deliberate elevation of analytical flexibility to competitive strategy.

In 2007, Nokia held approximately half of the global smartphone market. It was celebrated in management literature as an exemplar of strategic agility. Its CEO stated publicly to a Finnish magazine that year: "Being fast is significantly more important than foreseeing what happens in the market. This is our key competitive advantage."

That logic seemed defensible. Digital markets are not stable; they constantly shift under pressure from new entrants, technological change, platform dynamics, and customer behaviour that nobody predicted accurately. If foreseeing is unreliable, the thinking goes, then react faster than everyone else. Agility becomes the strategy.

But this conflates two different problems. Agility as a methodology, consisting of sprint cycles, iterative process frameworks, and scrum ceremonies, was built to address a specific constraint: how to build faster and with less waste when requirements change. It is a process improvement, not a causal model. It tells you how to execute more efficiently. It does not tell you what to execute, why, or what the connection is between the changes you make and the outcomes you produce. A faster loop is not a better model. These are different things, and treating one as a substitute for the other produces exactly the pattern visible in that quarterly review: smart-sounding fluency, paired with a fundamental inability to predict what will happen when something changes.

Nokia was not ignorant of what was coming, because in the early 2000s, Nokia established a research centre in Japan to study one of the world's most advanced mobile markets. The researchers saw clearly what was unfolding: cameras, applications, mobile internet, music, and mobile email on a mass scale. They documented it, and then they closed the centre anyway, judging the Japanese market too competitive to enter. So clearly the capability to see the future existed for Nokia, but what Nokia lacked was a model hard enough to vary, that it would force the organizational sacrifice the future required.

Instead, Nokia's strategic framework was built for rapid response: a flexible explanatory system capable of accommodating whatever outcome arrived in the competitive landscape. When touchscreens emerged, Nokia would respond fast. When software ecosystems became important, Nokia would respond fast. Being fast was the competitive advantage. The model did not need to predict. It needed to accommodate.

The problem with a model designed to accommodate anything is that it cannot compound improvements to causal models. Nokia saw the iPhone launch in 2007. The flexible framework accommodated it: a premium niche product, not a mass market threat; Nokia's hardware quality and distribution would prevail; the company would respond quickly.

Each of these was a plausible narrative. None was a falsifiable prediction. And because none was falsifiable, none could be broken in time to improve the causal model before the compounding that Apple had built, with the iOS ecosystem attracting developers, attracting users, attracting more developers, each cycle generating more data about software-as-platform that entrenched Apple's causal understanding, had run for years without competition.

Nokia's share of the smartphone market fell from approximately 50% in 2007 to around 3% by 2013, in just five years. Not because Nokia failed to see the future, but because the model built to accommodate any future cannot generate the hard-to-vary causal understanding that clearly reveals what needs to change before it is too late. Sacrificing flexibility was the sacrifice Nokia refused to make. So it never built a structural condition that could compound. In fact, with great flexibility and impressive agility, it crashed into the ground.

> ***Most organizations sacrifice causal rigour to gain explanatory coverage: the model that fits any outcome by adjusting how the data is cut.***
>
> ***The system gambit runs in the other direction.***
>
> ***A model that breaks and generates insights is the only model that compounds. Each failure identifies exactly what was wrong. Each cycle makes the next prediction better and the causal depth more rigorous.***
>
> ***After five years, the flexible model is where it started. The hard-to-vary model has reached a place no late entrant can buy their way into.***

The Limiting Condition: Slow, Sparse Feedback Loops

ASML's loop closes fast. A prediction about fab performance can be tested during production runs, then over weeks or months, and then refined against the next batch. The feedback cycle is short enough that the model improves continuously. The advantage over flexible-model competitors becomes apparent within months or even years.

Infrastructure investment, regulatory environments, and genuinely novel risk categories are a different beat entirely. A model predicting how a concession structure will perform across a 30-year asset life faces its first real falsification years after the investment. In new markets, where neither competitive dynamics nor customer behaviour is yet established, the hard-to-vary model will be demonstrably weaker than a competitor's flexible model for the entire period before the market stabilizes.

This is the limiting condition. Explanatory precision compounds most reliably when feedback loops are short enough to falsify predictions rapidly. In domains with long feedback cycles, building the hard-to-vary causal model will, for an extended period, feel like falling behind. The flexible model appears stronger, not because it is more accurate, but because it never breaks visibly or publicly.

The alternative is therefore not better. A flexible model that accommodates any outcome provides confidence that is structurally equivalent to having no model at all. It just provides that false confidence sooner. An organization running a flexible model in a long-feedback-loop domain will feel analytically smart for years before the domain's outcomes reveal that the chutzpah was empty, that it had been predicting everything and understanding nothing. A great proof of this. It is the distressed and under-performing private equity industry. The LPs were conned into paying 2% fees for a decade and are now often left holding a bag of illiquid trash.

The prescription is not to build the hard-to-vary model; the compounding will be fast. Instead, build the hard-to-vary model and be prepared to outlast the period when the competitor's flexible model appears more capable. The improvements will come. The compounding will come. The sacrifice is the willingness to appear weaker for longer than one might feel comfortable or rational about, in a domain where the feedback loop delays the reward. An effective solution for long-feedback-loop environments is to use higher-frequency proxies.

Macquarie's infrastructure investment business proves this compounding. Every transaction is treated as a structured use case that generates measurable feedback on the physical infrastructure asset. The causal model of how infrastructure assets perform across regulatory cycles, demand variability, political environments, and operational constraints improves with each deal, each deviation from prediction, and each outcome that breaks a prior assumption. The model is optimized to identify which components of itself were wrong and to use that information to make the next prediction more robust. Over the decades, this has become the thing no competitor can replicate, regardless of how much capital they decide to deploy. The delay is the price, but the compounding is still real and relentless. The moat is slower to build but much deeper and harder for a competitor to cross.

Think, Share, Discuss

The one question to bring to any meeting where an AI investment, a strategic model, or a major analytical commitment is under evaluation:

> ***"What specific outcome would prove this model wrong, and what is our mechanism for detecting that failure before it grows into a commitment we cannot reverse?"***

Someone running a flexible model cannot answer this question clearly because such a model has no clear falsification condition. The answer will be hand-waving like "if results disappoint", or "if customers don't respond", rather than rigorous. Someone who has built a hard-to-vary causal model can answer it clearly, because the prediction and its falsification are two sides of the same structural constraint.

Anyone can ask the question above, but only this chapter's lens explains why the inability to answer it is the real signal, and how it compounds over the years to keep committing resources to models that cannot be proven wrong.

> **SHARE THIS WITH SOMEONE?**
>
> I just read something that clearly articulated a discomfort I've carried around into every strategy review for years: the feeling that something is wrong with how we analyse our business even when the data looks thorough. The problem isn't the data. Most analytical models are built to fit outcomes, not to break on them.
>
> A model designed to accommodate any result can never improve, because improvement requires something to push against, and a model with no falsification condition has nothing to push against.
>
> ASML runs its entire R&D compounding through deliberate failure: every machine that breaks in a customer's fab identifies exactly which component of their causal understanding was wrong, which makes the next machine better.
>
> Nokia saw smartphones coming in 2002, had the research to prove it, and still collapsed, because their strategic framework was explicitly built for flexibility and rapid response to whatever happened, which meant their model could fit any outcome and therefore learn from none of them.
>
> The only model that compounds is the one that breaks predictably. The sacrifice is looking analytically incomplete in the short run. Every AI initiative I've watched fail probably failed this test first.

You can now identify the difference between a model that explains clearly and a model that accommodates anything arbitrarily. But a causal model that compounds inside one system faces a different problem when that system does not operate alone: when the mechanism you understand is coupled to mechanisms in adjacent systems that you do not govern. Understanding your production process with surgical causal precision while misreading the platform constraints around it cannot compound. The next chapter will show you how to architect creating loops across different paradigms, in a way that they reinforce one another to compound orders of magnitude faster.

GAMBIT FOUR

COUPLING ARCHITECTURE: CROSS-SYSTEM LOOPS

Coupling Architecture: Cross-System Loops

The smell hit him first. It was coal smoke, from about 50,000 breakfast fires, in the cold air of a city more than 500 kilometres from the nearest shore. It was October 1015.

The Chola ambassador had sailed from Nagapattinam a few years earlier, past jetties still wafting sandalwood and black pepper, where Srivijayan Buddhist monks shared the waterfront with Tamil merchants counting bolts of unbleached cotton at dawn. The Chudamani Vihara's spire caught the first light as his ship cleared the harbour. He would not see anything like it for several years.

He passed Kedah, that narrow strip of Malay coast where the mangroves smelled of decomposing vegetation, and Arab dhows floated alongside Tamil merchant vessels with the casual ease of neighbours sharing a well. Nobody in Kedah's harbour spoke the same language. Because nobody needed to, since the Malay harbour master's scribes recorded each manifest in a hand that blended Indian numerals with local dialects. The prices were settled in Song copper coins, as if the Indian Ocean were, in effect, a small Asian lake, a shared Mare Nostrum for the peoples of South Asia, South-east Asia, and East Asia.

In Guangzhou, the scale exploded: warehouses the length of paddy fields, stacked with celadon jars, pale green and cold to the touch. The harbour master's clerks moved through the docks like devout priests performing a temple ritual: each arrival was annotated, weighed, assessed, and recorded well before the ropes had finished drying.

Now in Kaifeng, it became clear that the Song capital was a megapolis of about a million people, most of them living within the boundary walls. The Chola ambassador's interpreter pointed to a long stretch of plaster: printed price lists on paper, updated daily, listing the going rates for 200 different commodities. The ambassador, mighty impressed, just kept staring at the prices for many minutes. He carried pepper, glass, and pearls among other niceties. He would return with 81,800 strings of copper coins.

Two empires had just met formally for the first time. And neither fully understood what the other had built. Yet, in many ways, what they had built, separated by ocean, language, religion, and every possible accident of geography, was in fact structurally the same thing.

Looking at that diplomatic moment, the obvious explanation seems to be the meeting of two military superpowers that dominated Asia. The Song empire was roughly a quarter of the world's GDP. The Chola sphere of influence stretched across large swathes of South Asia and coastal South-east Asia, representing considerable economic heft. Rajendra Chola had completed an epic maritime campaign that breached the Sunda Strait and sacked Srivijaya's capital. The Song held the northern border against the Liao dynasty through a century of intermittent warfare. Both empires could, and did, project lethal force and medieval brutality across enormous distances. But military power for territorial control in the typical occupation-based empire on the Roman or Tang model was interestingly not the engine driving the Chola or Song success. And the reason it wasn't, is deeply structural.

Military force generates broadly linear returns. It takes roughly one unit of force to hold one unit of territory. Every expansion of the held territory requires a proportional expansion of the military force holding it. The relationship between input and output is relatively constant, which means military empires face a fundamental scaling problem: the larger they get, the more expensive they are to maintain, and the more catastrophic any disruption to that maintenance becomes. Rome discovered this painfully; so did the Tang, and throughout history, every garrison empire eventually discovers it.

What both the Song and the Chola built instead generated multiplicative returns, not from one self-reinforcing feedback loop, but from five. Each feedback loop's output is routed as input to the others, so that improvement in any single feedback loop is propagated through every other feedback loop it feeds into. That routing is the cross-system coupling system gambit, and unlocking it requires understanding what each empire sacrificed to build it.

In That Meeting

You have been in this type of meeting: someone presents an AI deployment that will improve demand forecast accuracy by 15%. The ROI analysis seems solid, everyone in the room nods, and eventually the CFO approves the budget.

Six months later, the results are disappointing. It is a failure, not because the model is technically not working; in fact, the forecast accuracy has even improved slightly, but the operational impact is entirely negligible. The meeting participants in the room attribute this to implementation friction, change management failure, adoption lag, and other "cultural factors". The behavioural factors are always highly contextual, but the deeper structural problem is the real diagnosis.

What actually happened is a classic system anti-gambit. The improved forecast feeds into a production planning system whose management logic operates on quarterly cycles and requires cross-functional S&OP consensus before any deviation from plan is ratified.

The model produces better information at the signal's speed. The system that receives that information operates at the speed of bureaucratic committee meetings. The improvement was dead long before it crossed the departmental boundary, not due to friction or interpersonal relationships, but because of the structural incompatibility between the management logic that generated the output and the management logic governing the system that was supposed to act on it.

What you just experienced is a clear pattern in which systems are optimized independently, and value never compounds due to a lack of deliberately architected cross-system reinforcing feedback loops.

The Five Loops: From the Chola Tiger to the Song

Both the Song and the Chola executed a system gambit at the same historical moment, in parallel, with no knowledge of each other's institutional logic. Both sacrificed something tangible to enter a system whose architecture contained not one self-reinforcing feedback loop but five, and crucially, a routing layer that made the five loops mutually amplifying rather than independent. The sacrifice was the same in both cases, but expressed in different institutional forms.

The Song sacrificed territorial ambition and the military management logic that went with it. The Tang dynasty, the Song's predecessor, had been a military empire: cavalry superiority, aggressive frontier warfare, and command of the Central Asian trade routes that provided both material resources and strategic depth. The Song inherited that model and immediately confronted a harsh reality: they could not execute and sustain it.

The Liao dynasty held the north, and so the horse-producing regions were gone, and two early military campaigns to recover the buffer territories failed badly. The system anti-gambit, the locally optimal response was to keep trying: invest in cavalry, tax the population for war, measure success in territory recovered. Wang Anshi's reforms in the 1070s represent that attempt in its grandest ambition.

But the Song court declined the system anti-gambit. Instead, it paid annual tribute to the Liao of 100,000 taels of silver and 200,000 bolts of silk. It decisively diverted the capital that military recovery would have consumed into canals, examination schools, and commercial infrastructure, because you cannot simultaneously fund commercial infrastructure and prosecute expensive northern campaigns. The two management logics are mutually exclusive.

The Chola sacrificed garrison logic entirely. The dominant model of South Asian polity before the Chola was extraction through occupation: conquer, station troops, collect tribute, hold power by force. The 1025 campaign against Srivijaya is the most obvious example: Rajendra Chola assembled an army, attacked from the unexpected direction through the Sunda Strait, sacked Palembang, captured the king, took the jewelled war-gate as a trophy, and sailed home. No garrison, and no attempt at permanent administration.

You cannot invest in a temple's land endowment and simultaneously fund a garrison army from the same agricultural surplus. The trade-off for the Chola treasury was non-negotiable. Both Chola and Song sacrifices purchased entry into the system gambit. Here is what that system was made of, and what allowed them to compound simultaneously on five dimensions.

Loop One built the agricultural base. The Song distributed more than 30,000 bushels of Champa rice, a quick-maturing, drought-resistant variety from Vietnam, aggressively throughout its southern territories, alongside the construction of canal infrastructure and iron tools. By 1078, Chinese iron production reached an estimated 125,000 tons per year, a figure England would not exceed until the eighteenth century. More surplus fed more urban demand. More urban demand created higher price incentives for agricultural intensification. More intensification required more hydraulic engineering, which required more iron tools. Without central planning, the loop ran through market price signals rather than administrative commands, making it self-correcting.

The Chola ran the same loop through administrative intelligence: Rajaraja I's land survey of 1000 CE graded the Kaveri delta into up to 20 distinct types based on soil quality, irrigation access, and cultivation potential, then converted them into a standard taxable unit. The state knew exactly what each plot could produce, what it was producing, and what the gap represented in extractable surplus. The Chola and the Song used different mechanisms, but with the same structural property: compounding agricultural surplus that fuelled everything else.

Loop Two converted surplus into institutional legitimacy. The Song's mechanism was the examination system: Bi Sheng's movable type reduced book costs, expanded geographic access to examinations, intensified meritocratic competition, and continuously regenerated administrative capacity from new talent rather, than hereditary connection. A farmer's son who read the right texts could become a senior court official. This went beyond an ideological commitment to fairness, because it was a mechanism for producing competent administrators without relying on noble families that might develop competing power bases or, inevitably, incompetent heirs.

The loop: cheaper books → broader access → more competition → higher official quality → better-administered infrastructure → more commercial revenue → more examination schools → cheaper books.

The Cholas' mechanism for institutional legitimacy was the temple. The Brihadeeswara temple at Thanjavur, completed 1010 ce, operated simultaneously as a bank, an employer, a landowner, a public archive, and a legitimacy anchor. Temple construction asserted divine authority, and that authority reduced the cost of projecting military power over territories under Chola influence. Lower military power projection costs freed up resources, that funded more temples; those temples generated more commercial revenue through banking and land grants, which in turn funded the next cohort of temples. Both loops converted state investment into compounding legitimacy, making military enforcement progressively less necessary with each cycle.

Loop Three used military force as a commercial catalyst rather than territorial conquest. The Jurchen Jin's conquest of north China in 1127 cut the Song off from the overland Silk Road. The Southern Song responded by investing in maritime infrastructure: China's first permanent standing navy in 1132, not as a conquest force but as a trade route defence force. Quanzhou became the world's busiest international port. Song copper coins, exported through that trade, became the de facto reserve currency of East and South-east Asia, attracting more foreign merchants to Song ports, generating more customs revenue, and funding more maritime investment. A competitor port could not replicate this just by building a new larger harbour. It would have had to replicate 50 years of institutional calibration, and those 50 could not be purchased at any price.

Rajendra Chola's 1025 campaign against Srivijaya operated on the same logic. Still, it was timed differently: one military strike opened the Malacca Strait chokepoint, and then the merchant guilds occupied the newly opened space for over a century without further military expenditure. A Tamil inscription found in Barus, West Sumatra, dated 1088 ce, 63 years after the campaign, records Ainurruvar "500" guild operations in Srivijayan territory. The army struck just once, but the commercial loop compounded for more than a century thereafter.

Loop Four built symbiotic relationships with merchant corporations. The Song's hang guilds controlled market prices, represented merchants in tax negotiations, and maintained the commercial legal infrastructure that made large-scale trade reliable. The douniu joint-stock structure enabled passive investors to pool capital across multiple maritime ventures simultaneously; a mathematical worked example of profit-sharing among four investors with different capital contributions even exists from 1202 CE.

The Chola's Ainurruvar "500" guild operated with its own flag, legal code, militia, and diplomatic relationships with foreign rulers. The merchant guilds provided commercial intelligence, overseas permanent outposts, and endowment revenue to the temple economy. The path dependence was built structurally: the Ainurruvar "500" guild's network, traceable from the Tamil heartland through Sri Lanka, the Malay Peninsula and into Java and Sumatra, was developed over decades of operation under Chola patronage and protection. A competitor could not simply replicate it by hiring Tamil merchants, because it would have had to replicate decades of network construction.

Loop Five made every other loop more efficient. Song paper and printing made administrative records cheap, fast, and reproducible. By the twelfth century, Song officials seem to have understood the quantity theory of money, that currency value is inversely related to supply relative to available goods, and practised something approximating open market operations to stabilize currency value, centuries before the concept was formalized in Western economic theory. Commercial complexity generated financial problems; financial problems required intellectual solutions; intellectual solutions improved commercial administration; improved administration enabled more sophisticated and complex commerce.

The Chola ran the same loop but through granite stone instead. A granite inscription on a temple wall recording a land grant was simultaneously a legal document, a public record, an administrative instrument, and, of course, a religious declaration. It could not be easily altered, lost in fire, or discreetly revised. Chola emperor Rajaraja I ordered that when a temple was being rebuilt, its existing inscriptions should be copied into a book and re-engraved on the new walls. He understood that the inscription system was the empire's institutional memory and took explicit steps to prevent its loss.

Now, let's take a step back and view the full structure.

Loop 1: Agricultural Surplus—provided the primary material input for every other loop. Without surplus, there was no revenue for temple or examination investment, no treasury for naval campaigns, no economic incentive for guild expansion, no administrative capacity for systematic record-keeping.

Loop 2: Institutional Legitimacy—made the other loops governable. Without the examination system's meritocratic credibility, commercial regulation would have been applied arbitrarily and been commercially useless. Without the temple's religious authority, land survey tax assessments would have been politically contested and fiscally unreliable.

Loop 3: Maritime Protection—expanded the resource base available to every other loop. Each new trade route increased the surplus available for Loop One investment, the revenue available for Loop Two institutions, the guild endowment income for Loop Four, and the commercial intelligence available for Loop Five.

Loop 4: Merchant Guild Alliance—provided the distributed commercial intelligence and overseas presence that amplified Loop Three's route-opening capacity, Loop Five's intelligence about distant territories, and Loop Two's legitimacy reach beyond the core territory.

Loop 5: The Information Compound—made every other loop more efficient. Better records made agricultural investment more targeted, administrative selection more accurate, naval campaign planning more precise, and commercial contract enforcement more reliable.

This was one system in which five loops mutually amplified each other's output, instead of five independent loops running in parallel. The compounding of a single self-reinforcing relationship is impressive. The compounding of five mutually amplifying relationships is an altogether different beat. Not because five is more than one, but because each loop compounds the yield of every loop it feeds, resulting in ever faster compounding

THE ARCHITECTURE IN FULL

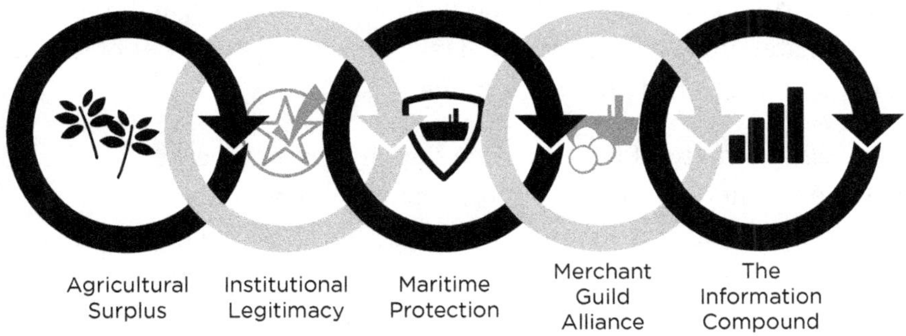

SACRIFICE	STRUCTURAL CONDITION	COMPOUNDING LOGIC
Single-paradigm optimization: maximizing returns within one paradigm's management logic, metrics, and feedback loop polarity. This management logic enforces paradigm purity for operational clarity.	A data routing architecture that closes loops between paradigm engines: Industrial production outputs improve Digital learning models, which improve Platform matching algorithms, which improve Industrial inventory positioning. Each coupling makes both coupled systems more capable per cycle.	Each cross-paradigm data flow enables decisions that neither system could generate independently. Better decisions across all coupled paradigms generate more diverse and informative data. Each additional coupling multiplies the returns of all existing couplings. The compound rate scales with the number of active couplings.

Amazon built a similar architecture over the past decades. The three loops are visible if you know what to look for. The industrial loop runs through the fulfilment system. Value is defined at the level of the repeatable fulfilment process: a standardized, low-variance sequence of operations that reliably converts inventory into delivered packages while preserving customer trust. This is important because selection, speed, and reliability are not digital properties; they are, in fact, emergent properties of well-designed, well-controlled physical systems.

In that sense, Amazon Prime and free shipping are not marketing innovations. They are throughput mechanisms: they smooth demand, justify fixed-cost infrastructure investment, and allow the industrial system to operate closer to its efficient frontier without tipping into instability. The industrial loop is the flywheel that the entire system runs on. Without it, everything else is brittle.

The digital loop runs through uncertainty reduction. Once software exists, replication and distribution are effectively free, which shifts the binding constraint away from output and towards knowing what is worth building, and for whom. Amazon's search, recommendations, personalization, pricing experiments, reviews, and behavioural instrumentation exist for one purpose: to reduce that uncertainty faster than any competitor can.

The engine of value in this system is the validated use case: a specific, recurring pattern of customer intent confirmed by observed behaviour rather than by planning. The desire to reorder household staples with minimal cognitive effort. The need to find the most cost-effective acceptable version of a commoditized item. The expectation of next-day delivery with high reliability. Each validated use case reduces uncertainty, improves future decision-making, and can be replicated internally at essentially zero marginal cost. Crucially, personalization at this layer constitutes systems control, influencing the system's operation directly. It routes demand towards items that can be fulfilled more efficiently, reduces the cognitive overload created by extreme assortment, and feeds higher-quality signals back into forecasting and inventory placement. The digital loop does not replace the industrial one. It guides and steers it.

Fulfilled by Amazon (FBA) is the platform paradigm's physical footprint, and the best proof that the three loops are genuinely coupled rather than merely adjacent. A third-party seller enrolling in FBA plugs directly into Amazon's industrial processes: its warehouses, packing lines, and last-mile logistics.

The seller does not need to solve the industrial loop. The platform inherits it, and customers receive the same reliability guarantee as with first-party Amazon purchases, meaning the platform loop's trust condition is satisfied without requiring each seller to build the operational infrastructure that trust demands from scratch. And because FBA sellers generate fulfilment volume, they feed richer behavioural data back into the digital loop, more transactions, more purchase-to-delivery signals, and more inventory positioning intelligence, which improves the industrial system's forecasting accuracy for every seller on the platform, including the ones who never enrolled in FBA.

The mechanism runs in all three paradigms simultaneously. Sellers gain industrial capability that they could not afford to build on their own. Customers receive reliability that expands the platform's liquidity. Amazon gains higher volume, more data, and a structural dependency. Once a seller's inventory is positioned within Amazon's fulfilment network, leaving incurs painful financial cost and operational friction. The industrial loop, the digital loop, and the platform loop are now running through the same physical transaction.

This is why FBA is especially difficult to replicate: not only because the logistics are proprietary, but also because replicating the coupling requires industrial capability, digital learning infrastructure, and platform governance maturity to coexist within the same organization from the outset. Most competitors have one. Some have two. No one outside Amazon has built the coupled, self-reinforcing, multi-paradigm system that makes all three loops feed into each other and compound.

The platform loop runs through interaction density under enforceable trust. In the marketplace, Amazon does not own the goods being sold. Yet it remains responsible for the quality of the experience, which means it must solve a problem that does not arise in vertically integrated retail: how to achieve liquidity at scale without eroding trust.

Amazon's willingness to remove participants who degrade the system, even when doing so reduces short-term growth, is not a policy choice. It is the structural requirement for the platform loop to run successfully. Liquidity without governance in the platform paradigm is a destabilizing force, not a moat.

Amazon Advertising illustrates this well: it is a system built on purchase intent that monetizes interactions without disrupting trust, because it is grounded in observed behaviour rather than inferred demographics. It works because the digital loop has already generated the behavioural insights that make advertising relevant rather than simply extractive, as in traditional retail.

The digital loop's output, comprising validated use cases, behavioural predictions, and demand signals, feeds directly into the industrial loop's inputs: forecasting, inventory placement, and capacity allocation. Better prediction means inventory is positioned closer to where demand will materialize before it appears. Industrial reliability, in turn, stabilizes the platform trust that makes the marketplace work: a seller on Amazon Marketplace can offer Prime delivery precisely because Amazon's industrial process handles fulfilment, so the platform inherits the industrial loop's reliability without requiring sellers to replicate it. Platform volume then generates richer behavioural data, which feeds back into the digital loop, improving industrial forecasting and further stabilizing the platform.

The loop structure: industrial reliability → platform trust → interaction density → behavioural data → digital learning → industrial accuracy → industrial reliability.

Prime is the unifying mechanism underlying this coupled architecture. It is simultaneously a demand-shaping instrument for the industrial system, a behavioural data generator for the digital system, and a trust signal for the platform. A Prime subscriber generates richer longitudinal data than a casual purchaser: their repeat behaviour under a commitment mechanism produces the kind of signal quality that improves prediction across all three loops simultaneously. Prime does not belong to a single paradigm; it unifies by routing across all three.

Amazon Web Services (**AWS**) productizes and makes available to the outside world the infrastructure underlying this routing layer. It did not originate as a market-facing product. It emerged from Amazon's internal need to solve a hard problem: how to provision compute, storage, and networking resources reliably and elastically for its own rapidly growing digital operations. Infrastructure had become similar to a physical transformation chain, governed by capacity planning, utilization, reliability, and variability, all industrial paradigm constraints expressed in digital form. By standardizing its internal infrastructure into modular services, Amazon reduced internal friction, accelerated learning, and improved system reliability, while keeping complexity bounded through modularization. The platform layer, with APIs, developer ecosystems, and third-party integrations, then emerged from the external exposure of what the internal routing had already built. AWS functions as a diversification play in which an internal coupling architecture is productized and monetized externally.

This is fundamentally why Amazon forces competitors to fight across all three paradigms simultaneously, which is strategically exhausting for any competitor, in a way that single-paradigm competition is not. Retailers fight on price, optimizing the industrial loop. Start-ups fight for user experience by optimizing the digital loop. Marketplaces fight for liquidity, optimizing the platform loop.

Each strategy can succeed within its paradigm. But none can replicate what Amazon has built, because it is not a single loop. It is the cross-system architecture that couples each loop's output to the next loop's input, making the next loop's cycle more productive. The compounding is not additive across the three paradigms. It is multiplicative because the routing layer closes the feedback loop between them, and a competitor without that coupled cross-system architecture is not running a slower version of the same system; instead, any competitor is running a structurally inferior system that can only compound the slowdown.

Former Amazon executive Seth Dallaire has, over the past years, built similar reinforcing cross-system loops at Walmart, resulting in impressive growth and value compounding. So, especially for legacy companies in traditional sectors that already have an established industrial paradigm, building cross-system, reinforcing feedback loops within the digital and platform paradigms is realistically achievable and a great opportunity.

> *Five independent loops compound additively.*
>
> *Five deliberately coupled loops compound multiplicatively, because each loop's output is routed as input to the others, so every improvement in any one loop propagates through every loop it feeds.*
>
> *The sacrifice is not resources: it is the management logic that optimizes any single loop in isolation, which is precisely the logic the routing layer requires you to abandon.*

A Paradox and Limiting Condition

Every system gambit contains its own eventual limiting condition. Not because the system gambit was wrong in any way, but because the architecture that made the system compound successfully under one set of conditions makes it rigid under another. The property that makes a coupled loop hard to break from the outside is the same property that makes it hard to change or reform from the inside.

The Song's complication was military. Three centuries of commercial management logic produced brilliant administrators and no institutional capacity for military command. The examination selected for mastery of the classical canon, and so it did not select for strategic military competence. When the Jurchen Jin pushed south in 1127, the Song lost the north. They lost the north not because they lacked resources, but because they had never developed the doctrine, the officer culture, or the strategic judgment that a state organized around military excellence would have. In fact, the commercial loops continued running brilliantly in the south, as proven by the fact that Hangzhou became the world's largest city, and maritime trade at Quanzhou even reached its peak.

But when the Mongols came, they dismantled everything in one fell swoop. They broke the Grand Canal. They destroyed the cities where commercial concentration had generated the surplus that the system ran on. The loops that had compounded for three centuries because a military force destroyed the physical substrate they ran on the Song had no institutional capacity whatsoever to repel.

The Chola's complication was different. The caste-based social structure that enabled all five loops to operate efficiently under stable conditions rendered the system unable to reallocate resources when external conditions changed. The Vellalar caste administered agriculture. The Brahmins administered the temples. The merchant guilds were trading extensively across South-east Asia. Each loop's efficiency depended on these groups performing their assigned functions. Efficiency required specialization; specialization required hereditary assignment; hereditary assignment precluded the reallocation of talent that changing military conditions eventually required.

When the Pandya dynasty's military pressure intensified in the early thirteenth century, the Chola system needed exceptional military commanders. The hereditary warrior caste produced what it produced, and it proved far from exceptional. There was no mechanism to recruit talent from outside it because the management logic of hereditary role assignment, which made the other loops work, was structurally antagonistic to meritocratic promotion. Just like the Song's examination system could not be reformed to select for different skills. The Cholas' hereditary structure could not be reformed without dismantling the caste logic that underpinned the entire institutional architecture.

Both complications have the same structural origin. A self-reinforcing loop, by definition, resists disruption. Its output feeds its input. The same path dependence that makes it hard to replicate from the outside makes it hard to change from the inside. And every loop that has been running long enough eventually encounters a new environmental condition its architecture was simply not built to handle.

Solving that problem requires a new gambit: sacrificing a currently successful position to enter a new system with a different loop structure. Neither empire managed to execute a second gambit before the external conditions arrived that would have required one. The loops that compound also tend to ossify over time. That is not a system design flaw. It is fundamentally the structural consequence of compounding itself.

Think, Share, Discuss

The one question to bring to any AI investment committee:

> ***"What does this system's output feed into, and does the receiving system's management logic allow it to act on what we're sending it?***

Most meeting rooms will interpret this as a question about integration. But this is a question about management logic across paradigm boundaries. The distinction determines whether you are building a coupling architecture that compounds or just improving a single loop.

Not the coupling architecture is built. The loops are running. Each loop feeds into the next, and the returns compound. But something has changed in a way the architecture wasn't designed for. The loops now generate information and decision opportunities faster than the centre can process them. The binding constraint has moved. It is no longer a matter of whether the loops are connected. It is whether the people closest to each loop have the causal model required to act on what the loops are telling them, without waiting for a decision to travel up the hierarchy and back down. What does it cost to distribute the understanding of how they work?

SHARE THIS WITH SOMEONE?

I've been trying to articulate why some AI investments compound and others flatten out at roughly where they started, and I think I finally have the structural explanation. It isn't about the AI. It's about whether a coupling layer exists across paradigms. An improvement that runs inside one paradigm runs in one loop. An improvement whose outputs are deliberately routed into a different paradigm's decision-making, like for example industrial outputs feeding digital learning, or digital learning routing into platform governance, runs in a coupled system.

Coupled systems don't add returns, they multiply them. The Song and the Chola each built five mutually amplifying loops eight centuries ago, and the architecture is structurally identical to what Amazon built. The sacrifice required is accepting that each loop's management logic will periodically conflict with the others' metrics, and building the routing layer anyway. Every AI investment I've seen that felt somehow insufficient probably failed this test.

GAMBIT FIVE

DECISION CLOCK SPEED: CAUSAL DECENTRALIZATION

Decision Clock Speed: Causal Decentralization

The summer that Ahmadnagar capitulated, the Deccan plateau smelled intensely of horses. The horses of around 50,000 imperial soldiers, the cavalry mounts and pack animals, as well as, of course, the war elephants of the largest army the subcontinent had seen in generations, camped on the plateau's edge for months before the gates of the mighty fort finally opened and let in the invaders.

The Mughal army carried its own micro-climate with it: the ammonia stench of latrines, the heavy huskiness of grain stores needed to feed an army the size of a roving city, the pungent smell of harness leather and gun oil, and the annoying smoke of cooking fires that burn non-stop when you have to feed so many mouths. By the time the Mughal troops entered Ahmadnagar in the summer of 1600, the townspeople had already been smelling them for weeks on end.

The fort's walls of black Deccan basalt, the ancient volcanic rock that gave the plateau its brutal, heat-absorbing character, were still pockmarked by imperial artillery fire. Chand Bibi, the regent and de facto ruler, who had held those walls through two sieges with bold, disciplined audacity, was dead. She had been killed by her own courtiers in the final days, stabbed in her quarters by men who accused her of negotiating treason. The real treason was yet to unfold over the coming months. So the grief was still fresh in the air when the Mughal cavalry rode victorious into the city fort.

The sultan was less than eight years old. He was in chains. The nobles of the Nizam Shahi dynasty came into the Mughal camp in the days that followed. Each arrived with gifts: rolls of silk, imported horses, letters composed in the sophisticated Persian that Akbar's court required from those seeking its favour. Each performed the prescribed submission ritual. In return, each received the thing everyone with any power on the Deccan plateau could have wished for: a title, a salary, a position in the imperial apparatus, and, honestly, the one thing that mattered most in that moment—the right to stay alive.

The rationale behind these capitulations was pretty straightforward. The Mughals won direct engagements. They also knew how to win attrition campaigns. They, of course, dominated the resource game by orders of magnitude. They had absorbed every kingdom from Kabul in the west to Bengal in the east, and their court was sophisticated enough to find some use for anyone who came bearing loyalty and competence. Akbar's offer to the foes of the empire was clear and well-known: submit and be absorbed; resist and be decimated.

Resistance required soldiers. Soldiers required money, and money required territory. The Mughals now held most of the territory. For a Deccani nobleman with estates, dependents, a family to protect, and the memory of Chand Bibi's bloody end still brutally fresh in their memory, the path forward was not much of a choice, really. They were not necessarily cowards; they were just rational political operators reacting to a new reality.

In this unfolding scene, one man stood out. By then, his name had been Malik Ambar for many years. However, he had been born Chapu, in the Ethiopian highlands, sold into slavery as a boy, passed through the hands of Arab traders and several masters across the Islamic world from southern Arabia to Baghdad, before eventually arriving in the Deccan.

Malik Ambar was 52 years old, in great physical shape, and had decades of experience spanning the military, the economy, and government administration. He commanded roughly 7,000 veteran soldiers: the survivors of a Nizam Shahi army that no longer had a Nizam to fight for. They were loyal only to him personally and were waiting to see what he would do next.

Malik Ambar had no throne. He held no territory, now that Ahmadnagar had fallen. His only claim was loyalty: the soldier's loyalty that had to be earned with each campaign and re-earned with the next campaign, year after year. Everything else, every formal symbol of his authority, had evaporated with the opening of the Ahmadnagar fort gates.

From afar, he had stealthily watched the procession of submissive nobles into the Mughal camp for days. He understood their political calculation. In fact, he had made similar calculations himself, earlier in his career, when survival required it. But on this occasion, he did not join the procession.

What he understood, standing on the edge of the ridge, watching the fluttering banners of the imperial army planted in the city his masters had defended valiantly, was something the Mughal commanders, reviewing the surrenders from their command post, could not yet see.

The Deccan was a harsh territory. Unlike the plains around Delhi that the Mughals were most familiar with, the Deccan was a ruthless, intricate web of tricky topography: distances between waterholes were constantly in flux, the ridgelines that turned a road into a trap, and the seasonal rivers that changed their flow during the rainy season between August and December.

Ambar looked at this and made a unique calculation nobody around him had even thought about. The plateau is not a prison or even a trap. It is a clock. And that clock runs very differently for a system that does not require information to reach the centre before any decisions can be made. Malik Ambar already knew that the clock was ticking, and he also knew that he was uniquely placed to make it tick even faster, much, much faster.

Beyond Guerrilla Warfare

Bargigiri is the mobile guerrilla doctrine that the Marathas later codified and used to harass the Mughals for another century after Malik Ambar's death. As a result, Malik Ambar continues to be venerated as a tactician of unusual genius: a man who happened to combine extraordinary personal authority with exceptional knowledge of terrain. In many ways, it might be claimed, a brilliant improvisation for a lost cause. But this reading of history entirely misses the decision-clock-speed system gambit that Malik Ambar brilliantly executed.

Ambar did not build a set of guerrilla tactics. He built a structural advantage into a new system, designed to defeat the gigantic Mughal army. The deliberate sacrifice was the cities, the fortresses, and the external legitimacy of centralized command. What it unlocked for him was a special structural property that he could now leverage: a decision-cycle loop running deep within the Mughal decision-cycle loop. Embedded and significantly faster. In many ways, this was an early precursor to the "Observe, Orient, Decide, Act" OODA-loop that U.S. Air Force colonel John Boyd formalized and popularized starting in the mid 1970, when studying why air-to-air dogfights during the Korean War, were consistently won by American fighter pilots typically flying F-86 Sabres, which were technically inferior to the Soviet-made MiG-15s they were fighting.

Each raid his cavalry units executed was much more potent than just wreaking havoc at the point of contact. Every raid was critically an observation. The Mughal response revealed where forces were concentrated, which supply routes were defended and which were exposed, how long reconcentration took, and, most importantly, how command and communication times operated. That observation flowed back through the spy network to distributed unit commanders, informed the next strike, and generated a cleaner observation that informed the next strike after that. Each cycle improved the network's model of the environment. Each improvement made the next cycle faster and more lethal.

The Mughals had superior individual decision quality. What they could not match was decentralized decision frequency. In an environment that changes faster than a command chain can process, frequency becomes the primary compounding variable, not just quality. The system that makes faster decisions does not merely respond more quickly; it learns faster, and its model of the environment improves, while the slower system's model remains fixed for much longer. Malik Ambar's sacrifice didn't just leverage guerrilla tactics; it was built on a faster decision clock speed, embedded deep within the Mughal decision loop.

In That Meeting

You have been in this kind of meeting. The calendar entry says strategic planning, portfolio review, or go/no-go on a major initiative. The slide deck was built two or three weeks before this room was assembled. The market has moved since, and someone at the table definitely knows this, probably the person closest to the customer or the one running the operation under discussion. They are carrying information that arrived after the slides were finished.

The decision proceeds anyway. Because the process requires it. Because the process exists to ensure that binding commitments are made only when full information has arrived at the centre, and that requirement, full information before binding commitment, is the entire management logic of the business you are operating in.

The management logic Ambar dismantled on the Deccan plateau in 1600 is the one that governs your business decision-making structure right now. What you were feeling in that room was a structural failure: the decision cycle is longer than the window the environment provides to act on the outcomes of those decisions. The approval apparatus that ensures quality at each decision is the same apparatus that ensures those decisions arrive after their moment of relevance has passed. Better analysis does not help. More rigorous review gates do not help. They might improve decision quality while the environment evolves beyond the point at which any particular decision would bring value.

The standard response compounds the error. Escalation protocols. More information should be brought to the centre before commitments are made. More granular reporting and BI dashboards. All of it is a bet on decision quality. None of it touches decision frequency. What the environment is punishing is not the quality of individual decisions. It is the rate at which the system observes, updates, and acts, basically the rate at which its model of the environment gets revised by contact with the actual environment. The discomfort you felt in that room was legitimate. You were watching a system degrade right before your eyes.

SACRIFICE	STRUCTURAL CONDITION	COMPOUNDING LOGIC
Centralized command certainty: concentrating binding decisions at the highest hierarchy level where information is most complete. This management logic maximizes decision quality per decision at the cost of decision frequency.	Distributed governance capacity operating at higher frequency than centralized governance can achieve. Requires two simultaneous properties: (1) sufficient causal model distribution that local actors make correct decisions independently, and (2) decision cycle rate that exceeds the centralized alternative.	Each faster decision cycle generates more observations per period. More observations enable more model updates. More model updates make each subsequent cycle more accurate. The system becomes simultaneously faster and more accurate, note that the two properties that centralized governance cannot achieve together.

The Mechanism

The structural insight here is not that distributed decision-making is automatically always better. The sacrifice of centralized certainty, only when paired with a specific precondition, gives you a compounding structural property. Without the precondition, the sacrifice is totally useless. The precondition is this: you cannot distribute authority without first distributing the causal model that makes authority safe to distribute.

Decentralization discussions treat authority as the scarce resource: who gets to decide. The system gambit trades in an entirely different currency. It asks what understanding must be present at the edge, before a decision made there can be more than a local optimization that fails to add up to anything at the system level. Authority without that understanding is not decentralization. It is just a faster, distributed failure.

General Motors watched Toyota's Andon cord at its NUMMI joint venture in the 1980s. They interpreted it as a regulatory mode of system control: a tool allowing workers to detect quality deviations and stop the production line within predetermined parameters. The visible practice was framed as a ritual, and GM implemented stop-line authority at its own facilities.

The results were chaos or paralysis. Lines stopped too often because workers lacked confidence to distinguish problems requiring immediate intervention from normal variation, or not at all, because they feared the organizational consequences of halting production without sufficient justification. The practice had been adopted. The causal distributed model had not.

What made the Andon cord work impactfully at Toyota was the ability to arbitrate between two genuinely competing objectives, maintain production flow, and prevent defect propagation, based on a hard-to-vary causal understanding of how quality problems compound through a production system if allowed to proceed. That understanding was built through years of relentless prediction, relentless testing, and relentless updates to causal models when predictions failed. It lived in individual workers' minds and in the accumulated practice of making the causal model visible to everyone, rather than tacit. It could not be adopted by "change management" or PR announcements. Without it, the cord was either a source of organizational chaos or a meaningless decoration.

> ***Decentralized permission, without a causal model, is just faster failure.***

Traditional advertising treated attention like factory output. Fixed inventory made up of pages, slots, eyeballs. Long-term contracts are negotiated by humans operating on full information about pricing. Feedback was measured quarterly, by which point the campaign was already over and the outcome was known. High-quality individual decision, low frequency, slow model updates, with a central team making binding commitments for the entire system. This is the system anti-gambit in its purest commercial form.

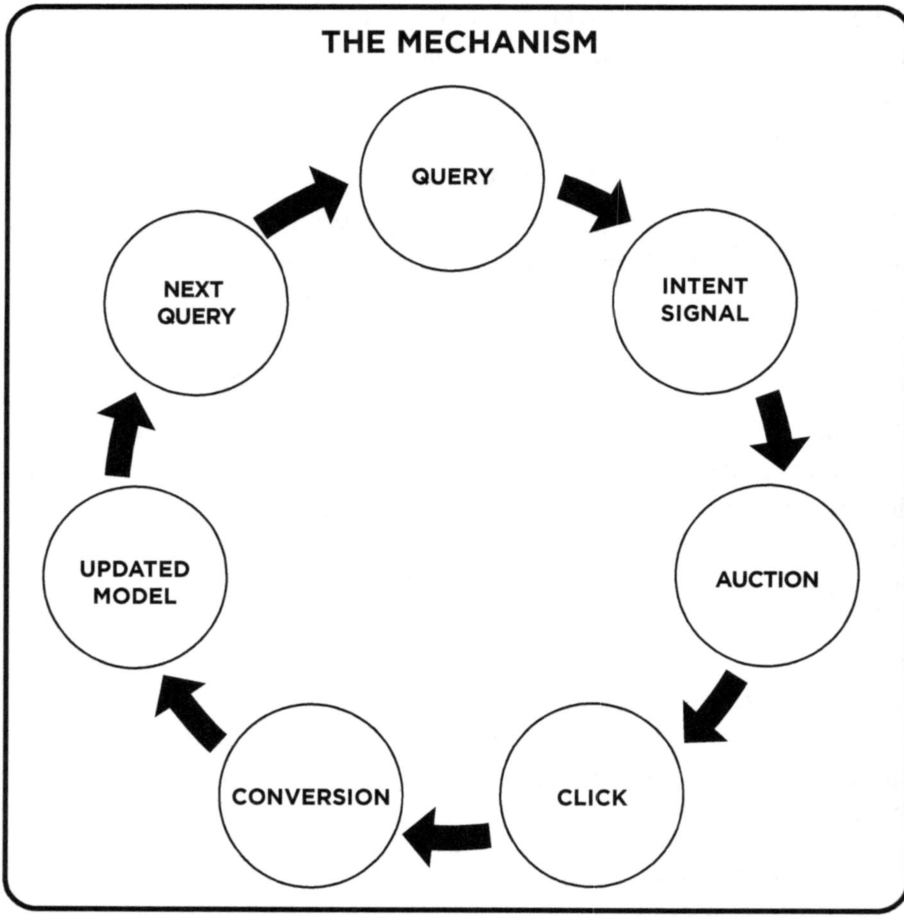

Google AdWords inverted the architecture entirely. Millions of ad variants competed simultaneously. Prices were discovered dynamically through real-time auctions. Every query revealed intent. Every click tested relevance. Every conversion validated whether an advertiser's model of what their customer wanted was accurate. The system did not optimize ads. Instead, it optimized the rate at which it reduced uncertainty about what people wanted and how much advertisers would pay to reach them.

The loop: query → intent signal → auction → click → conversion → updated model → next query

The feedback loop closed in minutes. Each cycle updated the model for the next cycle. The structural condition was neither better search or better advertising alone. It was a decision frequency that compounded while competitors were still waiting for their quarterly campaign reports. Google's competitors that prioritized privacy did not produce inferior search results. Their architecture was structurally inferior. They were running high-quality individual decisions at a low frequency against a system whose model was being continuously revised by hundreds of millions of distributed interactions.

> ***Decision quality does not compound alone.***
> ***Observation frequency also compounds.***

The bare causal chain runs like this. When the environment changes faster than the decision cycle, the quality of each decision becomes irrelevant if the decision cycle is insufficiently frequent. Frequency requires distributed authority. Distributed authority without a shared causal model produces decisions that optimize locally but add up to nothing at the system level.

Distributed authority with a shared causal model produces something different: each decision at the edge generates an observation. The observation updates the model. The updated model improves the accuracy of the next round of decisions. More accurate decisions generate cleaner observations.

The loop: distributed decision → edge observation → model update → more accurate decision → cleaner observation

This system not only acts faster but, critically, learns faster than its environment changes. It is what closed feedback loops do when the cost of running each cycle approaches zero.

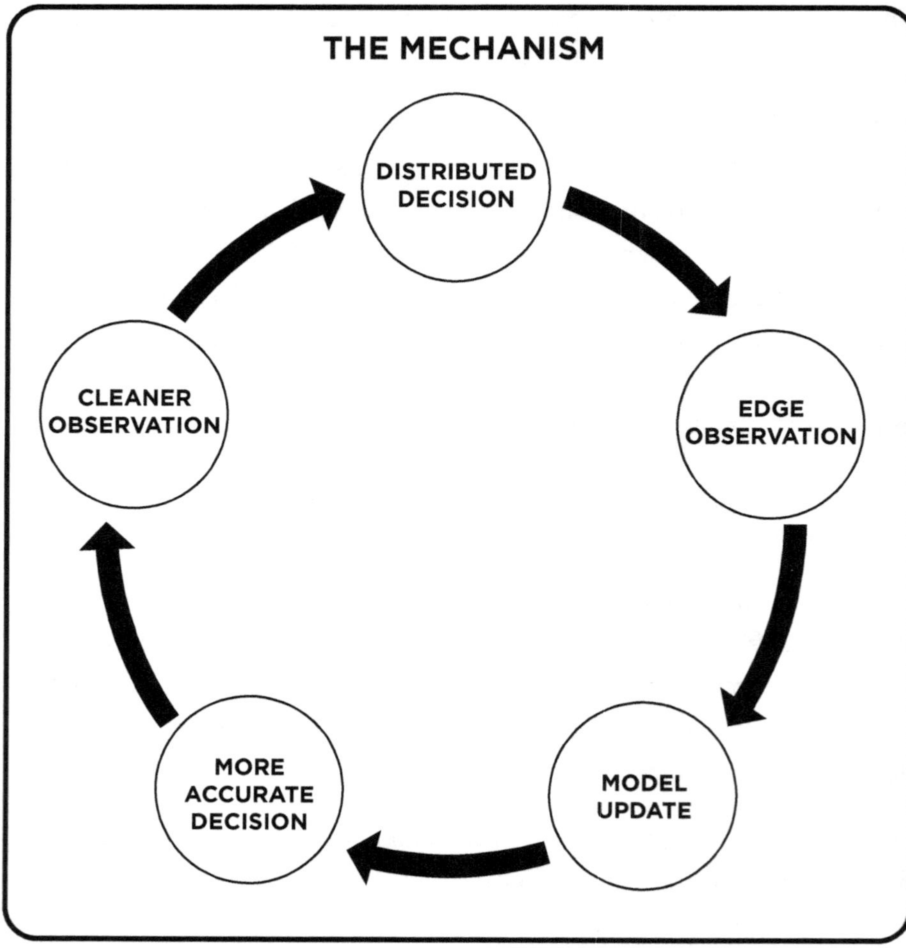

> *Some organizations distribute authority. The system gambit distributes the causal model that makes authority safe to use in a decentralized manner. Without the model, distributed authority is just faster failure. With it, each decision at the edge generates an observation that improves the next cycle. This system not only acts faster, but critically, it learns faster than its environment changes.*

The Common Complications

Organizations face the decision clock speed problem most acutely under competitive pressure, for example, when environmental change is accelerating, or the window for acting on decisions is narrowing. Structurally, it is the moment least suited to executing the system gambit, because building and distributing a causal model is expensive, slow, and invisible in existing metrics.

In such a rushed situation, operating teams will invariably make worse decisions in the short run as they learn, at high cost, what distributed authority is actually for. The investor tracking the current-quarter decision quality sees only increased costs, with no commensurate returns. The locally rational response to that signal is recentralization: bring decisions back to the people with the most information, reduce variance in local judgement, and protect the quality of each decision.

This response is not irrational because it addresses a real problem. The structural error is not centralization. An organization that centralizes because local actors lack a causal model, and then never builds and distributes one, locks itself into a permanently slower decision-making pace than its environment might require in the future. When wrong local decisions occur during model distribution, and they invariably will, the locally optimal response is always recentralization. That response permanently forecloses the structural condition. The system's anti-gambit reasserts itself at precisely the moment the gambit begins to work.

Robert McNamara's Pentagon during the Vietnam War illustrates the tragic and disastrous nature of the system anti-gambit. Decision authority was concentrated, and a single metric, body count, became the information substrate for centralized judgement. The soldiers at the edge had the accurate causal evidence: killing insurgents frequently and brutally, radicalized local populations, generating replacement fighters faster than the attrition model could kill.

This observation was structurally excluded from the central model because it lacked a revision mechanism. Officers who raised the issue of the divergence were removed. The system was optimized to improve its central metric, not to update its causal model when the metric diverged from underlying reality. That is not simply a malfunction of centralization; it is, in fact, its logical endpoint when the feedback loop between edge observations and model updates is deliberately broken.

There is a second failure mode, and Ambar proves it poignantly. He successfully distributed the causal model, but he did not distribute the architecture for updating it. The network he built outperformed the Mughal response cycle as long as the causal model remained accurate. When Ambar died in 1626, the network retained its operating procedures but lost the capacity to update the model as conditions changed. His son inherited the authority and the methods, but he did not inherit the mechanism for knowing when the methods had expired. Malik Ambar's kingdom fell within a decade of his death.

Shivaji, who built the Maratha state on the foundations Ambar laid, closed this gap with formal administrative structures that could systematically test tactical doctrine against outcomes and propagate corrections and updates through the network. He built the updated, revised layer that Ambar never institutionalized.

> ***The question is not only whether you have distributed the causal model. It is whether you have distributed the capacity to recognize when the causal model has expired and how it needs to be updated.***

Think, Share, Discuss

In any discussion where a decision is being made about governance, decision rights, or organizational structure, one question distinguishes someone with this insight from everyone else:

> ***"What causal model must we distribute before we distribute this authority, and what is the detailed approach for building, testing, and revising that model at the operating unit level before we move decision rights to the edge?"***

This question cannot be answered by someone who thinks decentralization is about trust, or agility, or empowerment. It can only be answered by someone who understands that authority without a causal model is dangerous, and that the compounding property lives in the feedback loop between distributed decisions and causal model updates, and that the precondition for the system gambit is invisible on any org chart. If the leadership team cannot answer it, the governance decision is being made at the wrong level.

SHARE THIS WITH SOMEONE?

The decentralizations that fail distribute authority. The ones that work distribute the causal model first, the shared understanding of why things work the way they do, and then distribute authority on top of it.

Toyota's workers stopped the production line not because they had permission to, but because they understood how quality defects compound through a production system, and that understanding made the decision obvious the moment it needed to be made. GM gave workers the same permission and got chaos, because permission without causal model is just faster failure.

Google didn't win advertising by making better ads, it won by distributing a model of user intent to every auction, letting hundreds of millions of daily decisions revise that model continuously, and closing the feedback loop so tightly that competitors optimizing at quarterly intervals were effectively operating in a different century.

The system gambit is not decentralization. It is building the model first, letting the model govern at the edge, and the part most gambits miss, distributing the capacity to know when the model has expired and needs to be re-architected.

Closing the loop reveals a harder problem. The causal model that governs distributed decisions will eventually be wrong, not locally wrong, but structurally wrong, wrong in ways no individual node in the network can detect from where it sits. Ambar's network ran quickly and learned nothing after his death because the capacity to revise the doctrine was never built into the structure. What does it cost to build an organization that can recognize when its own doctrine has expired, and is that cost one that your current management logic will allow you to pay?

GAMBIT SIX

SYSTEM ARCHITECTURE: STABLE INTERFACE

System Architecture: Stable Interface

The Champ de Mars parade ground, Lahore, March 1822. Dawn has barely begun, and the dust is already rising. The men drilling in front of Jean-François Allard are Sikh infantry recruits from the Punjab hills and the Doab plains. Their turbans are wrapped tight. Their beards mark them as Khalsa: initiated, covenanted; they are the warrior-saints of Guru Gobind Singh's tradition, a martial identity so intertwined with personal spiritual practice that even now, standing in rows, it radiates from each of them.

They are answering commands in French. They are wearing blue uniforms inspired by Napoleon's former army. The absurdity of the scene is not lost on Lahore's newswriters who filed reports on the two strange Europeans who had arrived in the city a few months earlier, describing them as "Ulur and Wuntoor", clearly foreign, initially even suspected of being British spies.

Allard is definitely not a spy. He is a former officer of Joseph Bonaparte's personal guard. He was promoted to captain and decorated with the Légion d'honneur. Wandering east after Waterloo because the emperor he had served for a decade was on Saint Helena and there was no more French empire to serve, he had come through Persia and Afghanistan looking for employment. His companion, Jean-Baptiste Ventura, had followed a similar trajectory: an Italian Jew from the Duchy of Modena, a Napoleonic officer with no Napoleonic empire to return to.

Of late, they have been offered employment by the Maharaja of Punjab. His name is Ranjit Singh, and he is 42 years old. He is one-eyed from the smallpox that took his father's life when Ranjit was 12. He was forced to take charge of a fractured Sikh confederacy, pressured from the west by the Durrani Afghans and from the south by the expanding British East India Company. In 1799, at just 19, he had captured Lahore.

In 1801, he declared himself Maharaja. In 1809, he had signed the Treaty of Amritsar with the East India Company: a treaty that fixed his southern boundary at the Sutlej River and, in diplomatic language, stated that the Company would destroy him if he crossed it. The Company had absorbed every other major Indian kingdom. The Marathas, Mysore, the Nawabs of Bengal and Awadh, they were all gone. Or shortly about to go.

From his court in Lahore, Ranjit Singh had watched this intently and come to a conclusion his peers probably had not: the Sikh cavalry tradition, which had built his empire and was the martial identity of the Khalsa, would not be sufficient against what was coming. His troops were individually brave and deeply religiously motivated, but none of it mattered if the East India Company could field massed, coordinated infantry and artillery with European drill formations.

Across the Champ de Mars parade ground, Allard's recruits are learning to advance in formation. The commands come in French, then in Punjabi, then in French again. The lines hold. The spacing is perfect. The movement begins to look like what Allard has seen on a dozen European battlefields: massed infantry that could sustain continuous fire through rotation, advance without breaking, and, most importantly, hold the line under countercharge.

Ranjit Singh is carefully watching from somewhere in the vicinity. Because the Maharaja took personal interest in the Fauj-i-Khas from its inception and could often be found carefully observing training, what he was building would, by the 1830s, be described by the East India Company's own military observers as equal to any European force in Asia. The British will station half of their Bengal army, about 39,000 troops, along the Punjab frontier. Not to attack, but to watch. The Company that absorbed everything else in South Asia will, throughout Ranjit Singh's reign, treat Punjab as a mighty peer. And out of fear and self-interest, avoid trying to conquer it.

The Khalsa Vieille Garde

The conventional reading of what Ranjit Singh built is that it amounted to military modernization. He upgraded his forces to European standards, hired experienced Napoleonic officers after watching the British East India Company capture every Indian state that fought it conventionally, and his upgrade worked well enough to deter invasion during his lifetime. While factually accurate, this interpretation misses entirely the system gambit he executed.

Consider the system anti-gambit: the rational, locally optimal response Ranjit Singh chose not to make. The Sikh cavalry tradition had built his empire. It had raided, conquered, and held large territories. The Khalsa warrior, motivated by a spiritual covenant and disciplined by faith rather than by drill specifications, was extremely effective within the paradigm in which he operated.

The system anti-gambit was obvious: deepen what worked. Train more cavalry. Purchase and import better horses. Deepen the individual spiritual warrior tradition that had produced two decades of uninterrupted expansion and power consolidation. This was the correct answer to every question his environment had asked of him up until 1809.

The confrontation with the East India Company at the Sutlej River changed the paradigm entirely. The Company's forces were not braver or more spiritually motivated. They were structured differently: massed, drilled, and coordinated across infantry, cavalry, and artillery in ways that made individual excellence largely irrelevant to the outcome. The binding constraint had shifted. Excellence within the existing system's logic would not produce the capability the environment now requires. The system anti-gambit had hit its ceiling.

What Ranjit Singh built in response was an entirely different architecture. And the structural condition he built, the thing that made the Lahore parade ground something other than a military history footnote, is the system gambit in action.

In That Meeting

You have been in this meeting room, where someone presents a new capability the organization supposedly needs: a new product line, a new technology stack, or a new distribution channel. The strategic logic is unambiguously clear. The room agrees it is necessary. The conversation stalls anyway.

Not because anyone opposes the idea. But adding it would require restructuring everything else. The people who run the current operation would need to relearn their roles. The metrics that measure success now would need to change because they measure the wrong thing for the new capability.

The incentive structure rewards the existing system's logic and actively punishes the behaviours required by the new capability. Adding the capability means re-coordinating the entire system simultaneously, and nobody can afford to do so while the system still needs to function day-to-day.

What you experienced in that meeting room was, in fact, a structural failure of a tightly coupled system. Every component is optimized with respect to every other component. It runs efficiently precisely because nothing within it is redundant. Because everything has been merged and fused, and the few remaining interfaces are specifically optimized for the components they connect to, rather than being a general standard that can be plugged into.

The system anti-gambit is about further optimizing the existing capability. The current function is generating returns, the management logic is working, and the cost of re-coordination is real. This is not the wrong answer to the current system's question; it is actually the correct one. The trap is that it works well until the environment requires a capability that the current system is structurally unable to provide. By the time that becomes undeniably clear, the window to cheaply build the interface has typically closed.

The standard system anti-gambit response always compounds the error. Hire consultants to manage the change. Appoint a transformation committee. Run a pilot. None of this is wrong, per se. But it misdiagnoses the problem. The constraint is not the organization's willingness to change. It is the absence of the structural property that would allow change to happen without system-wide restructuring and re-coordination.

Understanding this changes not just how you manage what you have already built, but actually what you build in the first place. The discomfort you felt in the meeting room was justified. You were watching a system get better and better at the wrong thing.

SACRIFICE	STRUCTURAL CONDITION	COMPOUNDING LOGIC
Integrated optimization: building the most efficient possible system given current components, where efficiency depends on tight coupling. This management logic minimizes inter-component friction by coupling components to each other's current state.	A stable interface architecture where each component can be improved by specialists operating independently, without those improvements requiring re-coordination across the whole. The structural condition is the interface itself, the stable boundary that enables independent variation on both sides simultaneously.	Each modular component attracts specialists who improve it. Each improvement makes all connected components more capable without requiring re-integration. More specialists per component generate more improvements per period. Total system improvement rate grows super linearly with the number of active independent improvers.

The Mechanism

Every business creates value through one or more of five fundamental mechanisms:

- **Production** (transforming inputs into higher-value outputs)
- **Allocation** (moving resources to their highest-value use)
- **Access** (monetizing durable assets through time-bounded usage rights)
- **Contracted delivery** (executing specific committed work under negotiated terms)
- **Risk pooling** (reshaping risk profiles across participants)

These are not analytical categories. They are irreducibly different value creation logics. Each has its own engine of value, its own binding constraint, its own clock speed, defined by the rate at which the feedback loop between decision and outcome completes.

This is where tight coupling produces its structural trap. When two value functions are tightly coupled, that is, when every component in one knows the specification of every component in the other, then improvements in each value function are forced to move at the clock speed of the slowest one.

The fast function waits for the slow one, as the slow one creates drag on the fast. Neither compound occurs at its natural rate. Add more functions and the drag compounds too. Instead of accumulating momentum, the system only accumulates mass by slowing down. Tight coupling is efficient because it eliminates redundancy. But it is brittle because it fuses clock speeds that should, in fact, run independently.

> ***Efficiency in itself is not a meaningful goal for a business to pursue from a systems perspective, because the gains of efficiency are immediate but temporary, and the costs are systemic and can effectively kill future compounding.***

The management logic antagonism is evident: you cannot simultaneously optimize tight-coupling efficiency and build stable interfaces because the two logics require opposing information architectures. Tight coupling requires every component to know every other component's specification: total internal visibility. Building a stable interface requires each component to know only the interface specification and nothing beyond it: deliberate internal opacity. They are structurally incompatible. You cannot edge towards one while maintaining the other. Every half-measure produces the worst of both worlds: efficiency degraded by the overhead of building interfaces that are not standardized enough to enable genuinely independent improvements.

The Fauj-i-Khas proves what an effective interface looked like in the early 1800s. The Sikh military at Ranjit Singh's accession was a collection of miscellaneous cavalry units, each optimized for its own sardar's command, own territory, and fighting tradition: tight coupling everywhere, with no stable interfaces.

There were already 1,500 European-trained infantry in his force by 1809, but they could not capitalize on their own. They initially only existed as isolated upgrades, not as nodes in a self-improving network of combined arms. No shared specification defined what "improvement" meant across all units. Improvement in one regimen did not propagate to others because there was no interface through which propagation could occur.

What Allard and Ventura brought was something much more valuable than better training techniques. It was the establishment of a doctrine such that any regiment trained in it could interface with any other, and any specialized officer could improve any single regiment without needing to re-coordinate the others. Allard improved the cavalry. Ventura improved the infantry. Claude Auguste Court, another decorated veteran of Napoleon's army, arrived in 1827 and improved the artillery, later supported by the American Alexander Gardner and the Italian Paolo Avitabile, among many other expat artillery experts. None of these expert expats required the others to pause. The doctrine was the interface. Each function ran at its own clock speed, and improvements propagated through the architecture specification to the whole. No need for endless "stakeholder management" meetings and change management workshops.

The best proof of this system gambit in the twentieth century has little to do with military force.

In 1987, when Morris Chang founded TSMC in Hsinchu, every reputed and serious semiconductor company in the world operated as an Integrated Device Manufacturer: they designed chips, built fabs to manufacture them, and sold the finished products. Design, manufacturing, and product strategy were tightly coupled. Each element was optimized relative to the others.

The system worked, and it was structurally incapable of serving external customers without creating competitive conflicts. If Intel built your chip, Intel knew your design. Trust was impossible by design. The tight-coupling logic made the external foundry service structurally incoherent.

Chang launched TSMC with a pledge: we will never compete with our customers. TSMC would make chips and chips only. No product designs. No rival releases. The huge sacrifice was not only the revenue those chip designs would have generated. It was the entire management logic of the IDM model: the logic that had made every successful semiconductor company so far successful. The pure-play foundry commitment was the interface specification: a manufacturing service standard that any chip designer could use, with the contractual and organizational guarantee that TSMC would never use their designs against them.

The compounding followed. Every customer who joined the network, like Nvidia, Apple, AMD, Qualcomm, Broadcom, improved their chip designs independently, and TSMC manufactured all of them. The volume and accumulated process knowledge from each customer's improvement cycle fed into TSMC's manufacturing process technology, making TSMC better at manufacturing for every other customer, simultaneously compounding rapidly.

Early customers like Broadcom, Marvell, Nvidia, and Qualcomm started with TSMC when they were small. Tapping TSMC's manufacturing was a significant reason for their success. "Not having us would have slowed down innovation in the industry," Chang maintained, because those companies would have had to invest in manufacturing capacity instead of R&D, or share their IP with a competitor. By 2025, TSMC served 534 customers and manufactured 12,682 distinct products. Each is improving independently. All connected through a single specification.

Throughout the same period, Intel ran the system anti-gambit. The IDM model kept chip design tightly coupled to manufacturing. It even produced genuinely superior chips for Intel's own products for years. Every attempted foundry service created structural contradictions: a customer asking Intel to manufacture their chips was, in effect, asking Intel's competitor to build their weapons. The IDM model's tight-coupling efficiency was real and durable. But the management logic of the antagonism between "we design chips to beat competitors" and "we manufacture chips for competitors without competing" cannot be resolved by organizational effort because it is deeply structural.

The Volkswagen Group's Modularer Querbaukasten (MQB) platform shows the same system gambit in physical manufacturing. Before 2012, each VW model had its own independent platform: tightly coupled to its brand identity and powertrain configuration. Adding a hybrid drivetrain to the Passat required restructuring the Passat platform. Safety improvements developed for the Golf did not propagate to the Audi A3, the SEAT Leon, or the Skoda Octavia. Each brand team improved independently. Nothing compounded.

MQB standardized the front axle placement, pedal box, and engine mounting position, with the same 12-degree rearward engine tilt, across vehicles ranging from the sub-compact Polo to mid-size SUVs. The sacrifice was brand team autonomy. Every Audi engineer, every Skoda designer, every SEAT platform lead now operated within the constraints of the MQB specification. What they gained was the propagation property: a braking improvement developed at one end of the product range moved through the specification to every MQB vehicle simultaneously. A new hybrid drivetrain, certified on the Golf, became immediately available for the Audi A3 without the Audi team having to rebuild its platform. By the tenth anniversary of MQB in 2022, more than 32 million vehicles had been produced across the group: each a product of independent improvement, all connected through a single specification interface.

The system anti-gambit failure mode is glaringly visible in Lidl's €500 million SAP disaster. Lidl operated its inventory management on purchase prices: the price it paid for goods, not the price it sold them for. This was not at all arbitrary, because it was based on decades of tightly-coupled optimization around Lidl's idiosyncratic operational logic. SAP's standard retail module used retail prices, which were incompatible with Lidl's approach, leading to antagonistic management logics: two different causal models of how inventory flows through a retail operation.

Adding the SAP system without surrendering the purchase-price logic required re-coordinating not just the software customization, but every process, reporting structure, and operational decision built on the existing logic. After seven years and €500 million, Lidl dropped the project and reverted to its original in-house system. Seven years without meaningful IT improvements at Lidl's core, and with half a billion wasted.

The trap here was not the technology. The technology actually worked in its own limited way. The trap was the refusal to surrender the tight-coupling efficiency of the existing system, to build the interface that would have allowed the new capability to connect without requiring the old system to be rebuilt around it.

ARM Holdings provides all licensees with an integrable hardware description of the ARM core, a complete software development toolset, and the right to sell manufactured silicon containing the ARM CPU. The ARM instruction set architecture, a stable interface, allows Apple to design the M-series processor optimized for its hardware-software integration, Qualcomm to design the Snapdragon optimized for mobile connectivity, and Amazon to design the Graviton optimized for cloud efficiency, all independently and on the same stable foundation. None requires ARM to change when they innovate. Each licensee's improvement increases the value of the interface for every other licensee simultaneously.

This is what the five value functions become once the stable interface exists: architecturally connected compounding modules. A business starting with Production, such as VW's vehicle manufacturing, can add Access (capacity rental across the MQB production network) and Contracted Delivery (bespoke variants built on the standard platform) without system-wide re-coordination because the interface specifies how any new function connects. A business starting with Access, like TSMC's manufacturing-as-a-service, can add Contracted Delivery (custom process development for specific customers) and Risk Pooling (capacity guarantees across the customer portfolio) through the same interface, with each function improving independently.

Without the stable interface, adding the second function requires rebuilding or restructuring the entire system. With it, the second function can just be plugged in. Every subsequent improvement anywhere propagates to every other function through the stable interface specification. The improvements do not just get added; they multiply. Each cycle is larger than the last, without a proportional increase in cost.

> ***Every tightly coupled system runs efficiently until the environment requires a capability its logic cannot add.***
>
> ***The system architecture gambit sacrifices that coupling to build stable interfaces between value functions, so each improves independently, every gain propagates to all others, and new capabilities connect at the boundary rather than restructuring what's behind it. The sacrifice is visible immediately. The compounding is invisible until it is unassailable.***

The Limiting Condition

The failure mode is structural and resides within the system's own mechanism. A stable interface enables independent improvement precisely because it does not change. Every party on either side of the interface, every licensee, every downstream function, and every external developer builds on the assumption that the specification remains fixed. The longer the interface has been stable and the more improvements have been built on top of it, the more costly any change to the interface becomes. The same path-dependence that makes compounding hard to replicate from the outside makes it hard to revise from the inside.

Ranjit Singh's doctrine interface proves this point. The standardized Fauj-i-Khas protocol was stable enough to train 30,000 soldiers and to produce a force that the East India Company assessed as a peer. But the cavalry "resisted reform almost entirely" throughout his reign. The cavalry had its ranks filled with recruits from the sardars of the irregular cavalry, allowing nepotism and corruption to intersect with the regular cavalry system. Because the cavalry doctrine interface preserved Sikh warrior identity in ways that infantry standardization did not, the reform specification that compounded for infantry actively prevented the same compounding from occurring for cavalry. The interface created the compounding and fixed the ceiling simultaneously. Where the interface was stable, improvement compounded. Where the tradition resisted standardization, the system gambit did not run.

ARM's current predicament is a different kind of complication on an industrial scale. The ARM instruction set architecture has been stable long enough for the mobile computing ecosystem to be built on it across billions of devices. That stability is its primary source of value. It is also why RISC-V, an open-source instruction set architecture that nobody owns, is gaining traction, not primarily because it is technically superior, but because it removes the single point of control from the interface. When the interface must evolve, the costs of having a single party control the specification become visible to everyone who has built on it, and they begin to value the option of an interface that no one can change unilaterally.

ARM's recent moves towards building its own chips risk alienating the licensee ecosystem the licensing architecture was built to serve, thereby revealing the limit condition. The moment the interface-holder begins competing with the interface-users, the trust that made the stable interface valuable begins to erode more rapidly than any capability edge can replace it.

Therefore, the complication is not about whether to build stable interfaces. It is about two separate requirements that the system gambit does not automatically satisfy.

First, the interface must be designed at the right level of abstraction: specific enough to enable independent improvement, general enough that the specification can accommodate capabilities not yet imagined. Too tight, and the interface constrains improvement rather than enabling it; too loose and independence without compatibility produces waste and overhead.

Second, the governance of interface evolution must be designed deliberately.

Who decides when the specification changes?

On what grounds?

With what accountability to the parties who have built on top of it?

Without clear answers, the interface that has been compounded over a decade becomes either too rigid, unable to evolve as the environment changes, or, conversely, too volatile, changed by whoever controls it, imposing high coordination costs on everyone downstream.

Ranjit Singh solved the first problem. He did not solve the second, evidenced by the fact that when he died in 1839, there was no institutional governance architecture for the doctrine interface he had built. The French officers began leaving. The compounding stopped because there was no mechanism to maintain and evolve it after the person who had architected it was gone.

Think, Share, Discuss

In any boardroom where a decision is being made about capability building, integration, or acquisition, one question changes the quality of the conversation immediately:

> ***"Can you state the interface specification, what crosses the boundary between these two functions, at what frequency, governed by what standard, and who has the authority to change that specification when the business needs to evolve it?"***

This question cannot be answered by someone who thinks integration is about cultural alignment, reporting lines, or shared OKRs. It can only be answered by someone who understands that compounding across value functions requires stable interfaces, that stable interfaces require explicit governance, and that the sacrifice of tight-coupling efficiency is only worth making if the interface is designed well enough to enable independent improvement on both sides. If these questions aren't answered, an integration decision is made without the architecture to support it, which would compound the problem.

SHARE THIS WITH SOMEONE?

I've been trying to articulate why some businesses compound across everything they touch, while others, even very well-run ones, plateau at the ceiling of their original business model.

The structural explanation isn't strategy or culture. It's whether stable interfaces exist between value functions. A tightly coupled single-function business can optimize its one engine exquisitely. It cannot add a second function without re-coordinating the entire system, unless it first builds a stable interface that allows each function to improve independently.

TSMC doesn't design chips, but every chip improvement by every licensee flows through the TSMC process technology and compounds TSMC's manufacturing capability. Volkswagen's MQB doesn't specify what individual models look like, but every safety improvement developed for any single model propagates across 11 brands simultaneously through the platform specification.

Ranjit Singh didn't drill every regiment himself, he defined the stable interface and let specialist officers improve each regiment independently, creating the only South Asian army the East India Company never attempted to conquer. The gambit is not about adding capabilities. It is about building the interface specification that allows capabilities to compound independently, and then building the governance to keep that interface honest when it needs to evolve.

The architecture is built: stable interfaces connect independent value functions, each improving without requiring the others to re-coordinate, improvements propagating through the specification to compound across the system. But stable interfaces only work when a governance structure defines and enforces them. Someone has to decide what the specification says. Someone has to decide when it changes, on what terms, and with what obligations to the parties who have built on it.

The businesses that compound most durably across paradigms are not just the ones that build stable interfaces; they are the ones that occupy the position where they set the specification for an entire ecosystem, that is, where their rules govern how everyone else's improvements propagate.

This goes beyond just owning an architectural position; it is primarily about building a governance position. It is a governance position. Who occupies it, before the ecosystem is large enough for anyone else to notice, determines who benefits from every improvement made by everyone inside the system, compounding indefinitely. The next system gambit is about who gets to set the rules.

GAMBIT SEVEN

RULE ARCHITECTURE: VACANT THRONE

Rule Architecture: Vacant Throne

The sugar harvest is underway. The cane fields of the northern plain are burning at the edges where the cutters have already worked, and the air smells of scorched sweetness. Saint-Domingue, 1800, the plantation at Bréda, where Toussaint Louverture was born enslaved approximately 57 years earlier, where he was freed in 1776, where he leased land and, for a period, supervised other enslaved workers, is producing again.

The plantation system had not initially survived the revolution. The great uprising of August 1791 had destroyed the plantation economy of what had been the most profitable colony in the Americas: 130,000 enslaved Africans working roughly one-third of the world's sugar and more than half its coffee had walked off the fields, burned the great houses, and begun the only successful slave revolution in all of history.

But the cane fields are producing now because Toussaint Louverture has ordered them to. His Agricultural Regulations of 1800 required the formerly enslaved population to remain on their plantations and continue agricultural labour. The regulations are enforced by military officers appointed by Toussaint himself. Workers who leave the land without authorization are treated as deserters. The plantation system is operating again under labour discipline that any French colonial administrator from 1788 would have proudly recognized.

Toussaint has even brought back the French planters who fled in 1793. He has made trade agreements with the British and the Americans: the same British and Americans whose governments held enslaved people and whose merchants had grown wealthy from the plantation system. The revolution was supposed to have ended.

In Paris, the abolitionist journals call Toussaint Louverture a traitor to his race. In London, the colonial press calls him an agent of French interests. In the American South, Thomas Jefferson refuses to continue trading with Saint-Domingue because the blatant proof of a self-governing Black republic is too dangerous to acknowledge. Meanwhile, in Saint-Domingue, the formerly enslaved field workers file back into the cane rows at dawn, supervised by Toussaint's officers, meticulously producing the sugar that funds his army.

No interpretation of this situation provides any moral comfort. The man who had proclaimed liberty for 400,000 enslaved people has restored harsh labour laws and discipline to the very system that enslaved them. His nephew, Moïse, who commanded the northern province, refused to enforce the regulations and was accused of inciting a worker uprising. Toussaint had Moïse arrested, tried before a military court, and shot dead. The workers who had supported Moïse were also coldly executed in the dozens.

The very man who was himself born enslaved, who had successfully masterminded and fought for liberation for a decade, who would be celebrated for centuries as the father of the first free Black nation, also ruthlessly executed men for refusing to make other men work in the cane fields. Let that sink in.

Whatever Toussaint Louverture was building, it was definitely not what it appeared to be from the outside. In July 1801, with the harvest completed, the trade agreements signed, and the military command structure fully loyal to him personally rather than to any French authority, Toussaint convened a constitutional assembly that included white planters and produced the constitution of Saint-Domingue. Article 28 named him governor–general for Life. Article 30 gave him the exclusive right to name his own successor, with the clause that the name remain sealed until his death. Article 77 sent the constitution to Paris for Napoleon's approval while simultaneously directing Toussaint to proceed with its execution across the entire territory, regardless of whether approval arrived from Paris.

Napoleon read the document and replied that Toussaint was "no more than a rebel slave who needed to be removed, whatever the cost". Removing him from power required sending his brother-in-law, General Leclerc, with

20,000 veteran troops, and then dishonourably and shamelessly betraying a flag of truce to arrest Toussaint personally. It is ironic that one of modern France's most prolific institution builders blatantly and disgracefully betrayed the flag of truce, one of the oldest institutions of humanity, to deviously trick and betray a brilliant former slave who had clearly outsmarted him repeatedly. Toussaint Louverture was then eventually secretly shipped in chains to a prison in the Jura Mountains, where he died alone and uprooted from his home in April 1803.

The revolution continued. Dessalines completed it successfully in January 1804. Haiti was independent. The conventional reading of Toussaint Louverture is biographical tragedy. A revolutionary who achieved the impossible, via a military liberation from three European powers simultaneously, and then lost his way. A great man with a fatal flaw. This reading seems coherent, but it is wrong about the structural question: what was Toussaint Louverture building, and did it actually work?

A good starting point is to look at the system anti-gambit he deliberately avoided. The liberation logic of the revolution was evident: reject the plantation system, expel the former slaveholders, refuse cooperation with France and other colonial powers, and declare independence. This was idealism expressed as a claim to high moral ground, based on the logic of the revolution.

But from a governance architecture perspective, it remained a position within the existing rule structure rather than above it. Declaring independence placed Saint-Domingue within the international framework governing sovereign states, which in 1800 meant a world in which France, Britain, Spain, and the United States wrote the rules by which other nations could exist. Liberation was the right goal for the current system of slavery, but not the goal that would be aligned with what Toussaint wanted to build as a durable system.

Every move that looked like a betrayal of the revolution's values was an embedded governance institution before any external power could contest the position Toussaint was building. Because Toussaint had moved to an entirely different system, he was building the position that would determine the criteria his successors would operate under, which meant, in the short term, sacrificing every criticism the current system had levelled at him.

The trade agreements with Britain and the United States set precedents: Saint-Domingue was recognized as an entity with the authority to enter into treaty relationships independently of France. The restored plantation economy gave the position economic clout, independence, and legitimacy. The military command structure whose loyalty ran to Toussaint personally gave it coercive authority. None of these was an arbitrary or disconnected policy. They were the three load-bearing columns of a governance architecture, each making the other more feasible and successful. Toussaint's compounding loop ran primarily through the legitimacy of governance, not just through liberation.

The 1801 constitution was the culmination of this system gambit. The document was simultaneously sent to Paris for approval and directed to be executed immediately without waiting for it. Built over 12 years, institution by institution, until the governance architecture was more deeply embedded than any external authority could remove without destroying what it was trying to recover.

The ultimate proof is Napoleon's response. The most powerful military commander in the world needed to betray a flag of truce, the most disgusting and shameful diplomatic violation in Napoleonic foreign policy, one that permanently damaged France's credibility with every European power, to violently kidnap a man whose only title was solely derived from the constitution he had masterminded. And despite that, the structural condition held: the revolution continued without him, executed and completed by the institutions he had built and the commanders he had mentored. Toussaint Louverture was not building the rebel state he seemed to be building: it was the Rule Architecture System Gambit occupying a vacant throne.

In That Meeting

You were in the room. Not necessarily this week, but maybe six months ago, or maybe even two years ago: the slide deck showed the competitive landscape, with regulatory requirements listed and industry standards presented as market conditions. The dominant platform's terms are identified as parameters within which options were defined. Someone was presenting option A versus option B, and both options assumed the rule structure as fixed by others in the background.

At some point during the discussion, as the Q&A began, you had a strange feeling of dissatisfaction. Not a disagreement with the analysis or confusion about which option to pursue, but something much deeper: the sense that the question of who built the standards you were treating as constraints, when they were built, and whether the position from which they were built was still occupied or had been vacated, was a fundamentally different question from the one the room was discussing. You didn't raise it because there was no section for that kind of question on the meeting agenda, and so, as always happens, the meeting discussion moved to execution.

The dissatisfaction you felt was legitimate. You detected something powerful: every rule structure has an author, and the authorship position is structurally different from any position within the rules. The entity that built the rules you treat as the environment was not optimising within the environment. It was actually building the system that is the environment. That position is not subject to the same constraints you operate under. It was available, at some point, before someone took it. And if all your leadership team is discussing is execution details, then they can never build or occupy the vacant throne offered by the rule architecture system gambit.

The rule-setting position is invisible during the period when it is most achievable. Before it is occupied, it looks like a governance obligation that no one wants, like a coordination problem that benefits everyone if someone resolves it, but benefits no individual actor enough to justify the investment. The certification body that would establish trust across the market has no participants to certify yet. The standard that would reduce transaction costs for all sides does not yet exist. The platform that would define the terms of interaction is building infrastructure that generates nothing measurable during the investment. The sacrifice period looks, by every existing system metric, identical to a failed investment.

The meeting room was asking the system anti-gambit question: how do we compete effectively within this structure? It is the right question for the system as currently constituted. The system gambit question, which of the constraints we are treating as fixed were built by someone who accepted a governance obligation their competitors refused, and which positions like that are currently vacant, is a different question entirely. It does not assume the current system structure as given. It treats the current structure as the output of previous system-gambit decisions made by others and asks which decisions are now available. Nobody in that room asked the vacant throne question. There was no section for that kind of question in the agenda. There rarely is.

SACRIFICE	STRUCTURAL CONDITION	COMPOUNDING LOGIC
Operating within the current rules: optimizing competitive position subject to the existing rule structure. This management logic treats rules as constraints to be navigated, not structural conditions to be designed.	The structural position from which the rules governing all system participants can be set and changed. Not the rules themselves, but the governing authority, the position that controls what the rules of the game are and can revise them as the system evolves.	More participants subject to your rules → your position as rule-setter more legitimate and more entrenched → you can set higher-value or more demanding rules → system generates more valuable outcomes → more participants join → greater rule-setting authority. Each rule cycle deepens the position's legitimacy and reach.

The Mechanism

The common structure is often this: a coordination failure exists that all participants share but that none can resolve individually, such as information asymmetry, quality inconsistency, a trust deficit, and a lack of a reliable arbitration mechanism. The actor who accepts the obligation to resolve it fairly, with neutrality, impartiality, and service to the system rather than extraction from it, essentially accepts a cost that provides no competitive advantage within the current system. Nothing measurable happens for a sustained period. But each participant who accepts the new governance ratifies the new authority.

And with that, the compounding loop kicks in: each ratification deepens legitimacy; deeper legitimacy enables higher-value or more demanding rules; higher-value rules attract more participants who need those standards; and more participants, in turn, further deepen legitimacy.

The loop: governance obligation → participant ratification → legitimacy → higher-value rules → more participants → deeper legitimacy.

The unique path-dependence is what makes the position durable in a way that ordinary competitive advantages are not. A better product can be copied. A better process can be licensed. But accumulated legitimacy cannot be purchased. It requires participants' ratification over time, starting at the beginning of the loop. There is no shortcut. Entering later with more resources does not replicate the loop. It requires running the loop from zero in an environment where the rule-setting vacancy no longer exists.

The system anti-gambit is the position every ambitious investor-operator already holds: optimize within the existing rule structure, maximise competitive advantage subject to the constraints as given, and accumulate as much of the available value as the rules permit. This is naturally not a mistake, because it is the correct answer to the questions the current system is asking: in every performance review, through every benchmark, in every competitive analysis that treats the rule structure as already given.

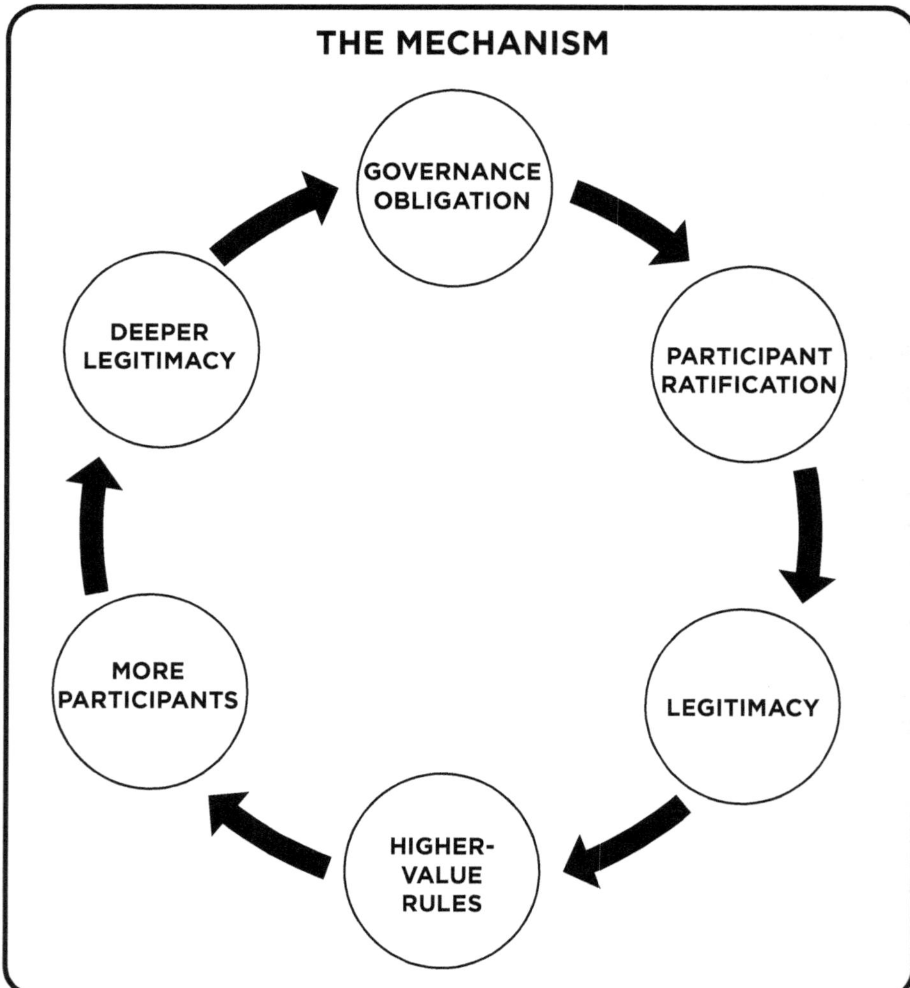

But the system anti-gambit forecloses the rule-setting position structurally. An operator optimizing within the rules cannot simultaneously uphold the governance obligation that sets them, because optimization entails exploiting every available advantage. In contrast, governance obligation entails subordinating advantage to system integrity. They are mutually exclusive. This is why the sacrifice the system gambit requires feels, from within the system-anti-gambit, like an inexplicable abdication: it is the abandonment of a management logic that is already producing decent results by every metric in the current system.

This structure produces one diagnostic implication: the governance obligation is not incidental to the system gambit; it is the critical structural condition at its heart. The moment the investor-operator begins optimizing within the position they have built, for example, by using governance authority for commercial advantage, favouring participants, extracting rather than serving, then the compounding reverses. Participants who accepted your governance because it served them begin to calculate and re-evaluate whether the cost still exceeds the benefit. Alternative governance architectures become attractive, and the vacancy eventually re-opens.

Edward Lloyd ran a coffee house on Tower Street in London from around 1688. He published shipping news, curated maritime intelligence, and provided the physical space where merchants, captains, and underwriters gathered. He refrained from underwriting insurance himself, positioning himself as a neutral facilitator who provided all participants with accurate information and maintained impartial records between the buyer and the seller. He could have underwritten directly, capturing the commercial upside of the market he was facilitating. He chose not to. Each underwriter who transacted at Lloyd's accepted Lloyd's as the legitimate venue and record-keeper for maritime insurance.

Each acceptance deepened the position's legitimacy. When two competing companies obtained parliamentary monopolies on marine insurance in 1720 and attempted to eliminate Lloyd's, they found that the market's participants had already built their commercial lives around the governance infrastructure Lloyd's provided. By an act of incorporation in 1871, Lloyd's gained the power to make its own bylaws, acquire property, and perform all acts in its corporate name. A coffee house that had never underwritten a single policy had become the rule-setter for global maritime risk, incorporated by parliamentary act with its own legislative authority.

In 1968, the US credit card industry was destroying itself. Banks had each issued proprietary cards in incompatible systems, mass-mailed indiscriminately to anyone on any mailing list they could find. Children had credit cards. Convicted felons had credit cards. Fraud was rampant, and losses were haemorrhaging across all issuers. Eventually Bank of America called its BankAmericard licensees to a meeting in Columbus, Ohio, to find a solution.

The meeting dissolved into what participants described as angry finger-pointing. There was no resolution. The coordination failure was structural, and everyone in the room could see it: every bank wanted to control the payment network, and no bank would accept a competitor's control of it. The vacant throne was invisible precisely because the problem looked unsolvable within the existing management logic.

Dee Hock was then a 38-year-old vice president at a BankAmericard licensee bank in Seattle. He was not a senior figure, and he had not been given any official mandate. When the Columbus meeting was at its most acrimonious, he stood up and proposed that the group study the problem more systematically. He had already seen what the others were refusing to see: the coordination failure was not a technology problem. It was a governance problem. No amount of better fraud detection or clearing technology would resolve the fundamental issue that competing banks could not share infrastructure controlled by any one of them.

Hock solved the governance obligation that every institution avoided. He designed a structure in which no bank would control the network. Competing banks would share governance on an equal footing. Bank of America, whose profitable BankAmericard franchise was the entire foundation of the system, would give up exclusive control entirely. The new organization, National BankAmericard Inc., formed in 1970, distributed governance among member banks in proportion to their participation volume. Hock himself held no equity stake. He built an institution whose eventual market value would reach hundreds of billions of dollars and owned none of it. That was the sacrifice:

the commercial position any single operator controlling the rails would have occupied, surrendered to accept the governance obligation that no operator who wanted that position could hold.

Each bank that joined added leverage by strengthening the network's legitimacy as a neutral payment rail and bringing its existing customers and merchants onto the system. Standard transaction protocols enabled by that legitimacy reduced fraud and increased merchant acceptance. More merchants attracted more cardholders. More cardholders attracted more banks.

Each cycle made the next cycle more productive. By the early 1980s, the Visa network had surpassed MasterCard as the largest payments system in the world. Hock described what he had built as "a corporation whose product is coordination". He would hold up a Visa card at speaking engagements and ask the audience who knew what it was. Every hand went up. He would then ask who owned it and how it was governed. Almost no one knew. That, for Hock, was mission accomplished: a governance architecture so deeply embedded it had become invisible infrastructure.

The economic structure of the rule-setting position is distinct from that of any position within the rules. Every bank that joined the Visa network was competing against every other bank for cardholders. Visa collected from every transaction, regardless of who won. Lloyd's collects from every marine insurance placement regardless of which underwriter won the contract. Michelin earns from multi-year "destination marketing" contracts from city and state tourism boards, based on every restaurant's dependence on its authority, regardless of which restaurant wins the award.

> ***The rule-setter earns from the game, not in the game. Within-system competitors fight for a share of what the rules permit.***

The rule-setter determines what the rules permit. That is the structural difference between the rule architecture system gambit and any form of competitive excellence within the existing structure, and it is why the compounding logic of the legitimacy loop accelerates in a way that within-system competition cannot systematically replicate, regardless of how well that competition is executed.

Apple's management of its Chinese manufacturing ecosystem between 2006 and 2020 is the clearest contemporary execution of the rule architecture gambit in business history. Patrick McGee's NYT bestselling book Apple in China is the ultimate account that follows the structural logic of what was actually being built rather than the story Apple preferred to tell about itself. McGee pulled back the curtain on a governance architecture that its architect had actively preferred to keep hidden.

Apple's sacrifice is gigantic: in the five year period, between 2016 and 2020, Apple invested over $275 billion in China, roughly twice the inflation-adjusted value of the Marshall Plan, training Chinese citizens en masse and building bleeding-edge manufacturing infrastructure and capability it did not own, thereby creating a dependency structure that it completely controlled.

In 2018, $13.3 billion worth of Apple-owned machinery sat inside factories bearing Foxconn's name, Pegatron's logo, and operated by several other contract manufacturers. Apple owned none of the factory floor space, but it owned all of the process.

The governance obligation Apple accepted was quality governance at scale: embedding the best engineers for months at a time in over 1,600 factories, designing production processes to tolerances that far exceeded automotive manufacturing standards, and training workforces in techniques that had no other customer. The sacrifice was not merely capital, but the logic of traditional industrial outsourcing, which trades control for cost. It was replaced by a logic that accepted the cost of achieving control without ownership. Full leverage over suppliers, with an asset-light balance sheet: exactly the kind of Goldilocks equilibrium that investors love.

What that governance obligation produced, over two decades, was something nobody in Cupertino, and especially in Washington, appears to have fully thought through: a generation of Chinese manufacturers trained to world-class standards at Apple's expense, on Apple's equipment, under Apple's engineers, who then became world-class technology companies in their own right.

The knowledge Apple transferred was task-specific: how to execute Apple's processes, meet Apple's tolerances, and maintain Apple's yield rates. Hence, what it could not prevent from being transferred was the deeper capability: the organizational discipline, the quality culture, the manufacturing sophistication that emerged from being held to standards most of the outsourcing world's factories had never even remotely attempted to meet.

By the 2010s, suppliers that had begun as low-cost assemblers were operating at an industrial complexity level that rivalled that of South Korea, Japan, or Germany. Apple had run the largest privately funded industrial education and upskilling programme in history, and its ambitious and hard-working students had just graduated.

The most telling testimony to what that education produced came from Ren Zhengfei, founder of Huawei, the company that would become Apple's most formidable Chinese competitor. When asked in 2019 whether he would support Chinese retaliation against Apple during the trade war, Ren protested. "Apple is my teacher," he told Bloomberg's Tom Mackenzie. "It's advancing in front of us. As a student, why should I oppose my teacher? I would never do that." He went further: "If there were no Apple, there would be no mobile internet". In 2023, with Huawei's Mate 60 Pro competing directly against the iPhone 15 in China's smartphone market, Ren was still saying he was happy to have a teacher he could learn from. By then, the comparison was increasingly between near-equals in the Chinese consumer market.

The structural condition Apple's investment purchased was rule-setting authority over suppliers and Chinese contract manufacturing. Apple's specifications became the effective standard. Suppliers who met Apple's requirements met everyone else's by default. Apple's engineers on factory floors in Shenzhen were embedding Apple's authority into the definition of quality manufacturing. Each supplier that accepted Apple's governance deepened Apple's legitimacy as the sector's rule-setter. Each new product launch that required a novel manufacturing technique extended Apple's rule-setting position into territory no other consumer electronics company could match.

APPLE FEEDBACK LOOP

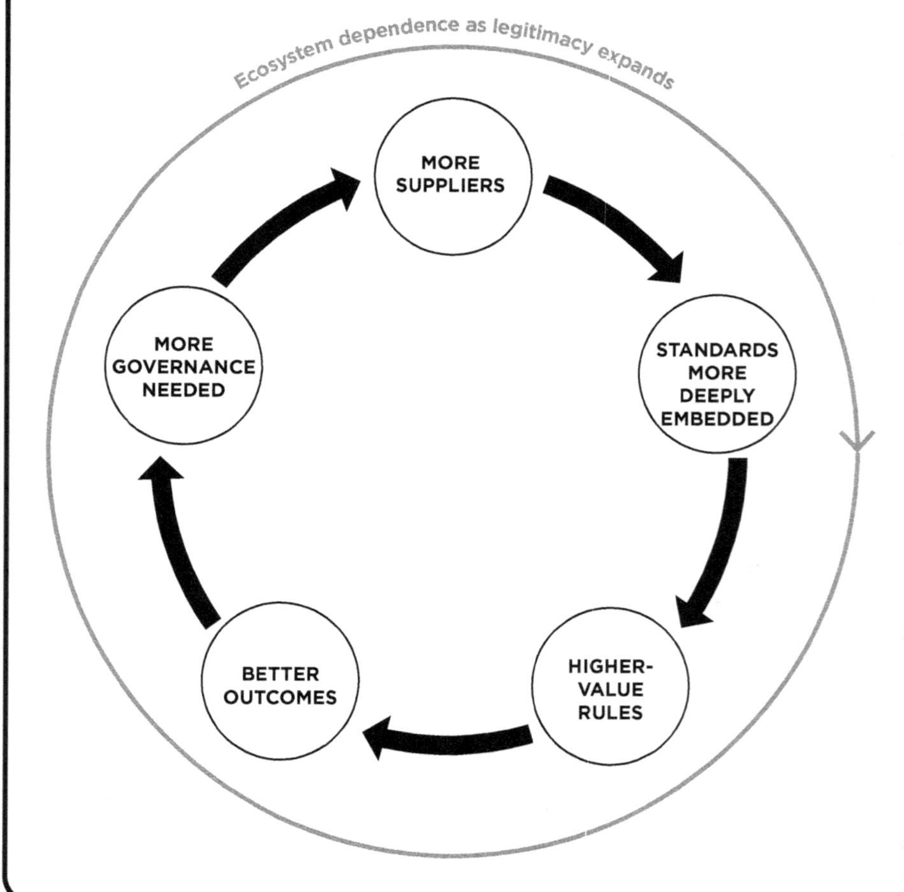

The compounding ran based on the feedback loop:

more suppliers subject to Apple's quality architecture → Apple's standards more deeply embedded as the benchmark → higher-value and more demanding rules tenable → the ecosystem produced outcomes no single-paradigm competitor could match → more suppliers needed Apple's governance to access Apple's volume → the position deepened further.

What Apple did not realize was that the Chinese Communist Party had been running a parallel Rule Architecture Gambit at a system level above Apple. Apple's more than $275 billion investment went beyond capital, creating a world-class industrial ecosystem that the Party could regulate, surveil, and leverage for its own goals. Each quarter, Apple's revenue in China grew, while its exit costs also exploded. Apple moved iCloud data for Chinese users onto servers operated by a state-owned enterprise. Apple removed applications from the Chinese App Store at the Party's request. Tim Cook called China "indispensable". That is the vocabulary and language of acceptance that only a participant in a new rule architecture would use.

Apple had built a rule architecture over its suppliers. Those suppliers had used it to build technology empires of their own. And finally, the Party had built a rule architecture over all of them. The compounding logic ran at all these levels, and the entity with the greatest system leverage was not the one whose logo was on the iPhone.

Cosimo de' Medici, for all practical purposes, ruled Florence from 1434 to 1464 without ever holding a title that accurately described what he was doing. He remained formally a private citizen, running his affairs through banking relationships that bound the Florentine elite to his interests, patronage networks across art and religious institutions, and credit lines that made him the essential financier of the republic during fiscal crises. He was charged with attempting to elevate himself above the rank of an ordinary citizen. So he accepted exile rather than fight the accusation, and returned the following year with increased admiration and status to a governance position he would hold for three decades, without ever holding a formal office.

Pope Pius II said of Cosimo de' Medici: "*He is king in everything but name*".

The management logic antagonism in Cosimo's case is the clearest example of the rule-architecture system gambit in action. The established logic of Florentine power was formal office-holding, with visible title, authority, and legitimacy. Cosimo's rule-setting logic required precisely not to claim formal power, because doing so would have made his authority contestable within the political structures his governance already transcended. The sacrifice was not simply a commercial stance, because it was also the social glamour that comes with any defined title and status: neither the honour of visible office nor the security of formal protection. The loop ran on the same principle as Lloyd's and Visa: each institution that accepted his governance deepened the position. The operator who claimed the position explicitly would have lost it. This was a sacrifice his grandson, Lorenzo the Magnificent, could no longer sustain.

The management logic antagonism is identical across every setting. The system anti-gambit logic optimizes within the existing rule structure, maximizes competitive advantage subject to the given constraints, and captures as much of the available value as the rules permit. The system gambit logic requires accepting governance obligations that competitors refuse, such as neutrality, impartiality, service to the system rather than extraction from it, and holding to those obligations even when they yield no quantifiable results. The two logics are not competing priorities; in fact, they actively destroy each other when combined within the same organization at the same time.

> ***Every strategy that treats rules as constraints is asking the right question about the wrong system. Rules are not natural features of the environment. They were built by someone. The system anti-gambit competes for a share of what the rules permit.***

> *The rule architecture gambit occupies the position from which the next rules are built: before others recognize the vacancy, through the sacrifice of within-system optimization, by accepting governance obligations that competitors refuse.*
>
> *Each participant who accepts governance deepens the legitimacy, which enables higher-value rules, which draws more participants, which deepens the position further. The most durable competitive position in any system is not operating excellently within the rules. It is being the entity whose governance everyone else must satisfy.*

The Paradox of Extraction

The failure mode is internal because it does not arise from a stronger competitor; instead, it arises from the management logic of the rule-setter's own success.

Toussaint's Agricultural Regulations of 1800 were the governance instrument that restored the economic foundation of his rule-setting position. But the decree that compelled enslaved workers to remain on plantations was also the first sign that the rule-setting logic was being displaced by extractive logic: the governance position was being used to extract labour value from the participants it governed, rather than to deepen the legitimacy that compounded the position. Toussaint built the structural condition correctly, but it could be argued that he was beginning to use it incorrectly.

The same mechanism is playing out in the semiconductor industry. Arm Holdings operated for 35 years as a chipless, fabless chip company, licensing processor architectures without competing with its licensees. Apple, Qualcomm, Samsung, Nvidia, and MediaTek all licensed the same ARM architecture because the entity that designed it would never use that position to enter their markets. The governance obligation was the structural condition: a chip architecture standard that the entire mobile computing ecosystem accepted precisely because the rule-setter remained above the competition it governed.

In March 2026, Arm announced the AGI CPU, its first complete production chip, designed to compete for AI data centre workloads. More than three decades of neutrality ended in a single product announcement. Design service partners who had built businesses on the assumption that Arm would never compete with its own licensees now face Arm as a direct competitor for the same customers. Tensions are already emerging in the ecosystem: partners are navigating relationships between Arm and its own licensees, and roadmap dependency is increasing as the architectural standard becomes something Arm competes on rather than provides neutrally.

The commercial upside that 35 years of governance obligation established might evaporate with a single extractive decision. If repeated, the aggregate consequence, made up of the erosion of the legitimacy that made the position compound, will follow the same structural path as every other rule-setting position whose investor-operator eventually chose extraction over governance.

The structural pattern is the same in every case. The rule-setting position compounds when the operator accepts governance obligations that competitors do not accept. The moment the operator begins optimizing within the rule-setting position, using governance authority for immediate commercial advantage, the compounding reverses. This is not a purely moral failing, but rather a reversion to management logic: the locally rational response to having built something valuable enough to extract from. Every individual decision to extract is rational. The aggregate consequence is the erosion of the legitimacy that made the position compound in the first place.

The governance obligation that built the position is the governance obligation that sustains it. There is no version of this system gambit that compounds without it. It's like slaughtering the goose that lays the golden eggs.

Think, Share, Discuss

In any room where competitive strategy, regulatory positioning, or industry standards are being discussed, one question changes the depth and quality of the conversation:

> ***"Which of the rules we're treating as constraints were built by someone who accepted a governance obligation their competitors refused, and which positions like that are currently vacant?"***

Neither half of the question can be answered by someone who thinks the competitive environment is a natural landscape rather than a built structure. The first half requires knowing that every rule structure has an author and a governance obligation behind it. The second requires the diagnostic capacity to identify a coordination failure as a vacancy rather than simply a problem. If the room cannot name who set the current rules, it cannot see what the next rules might be, who is currently positioned to set them, or whether someone is already setting them without anyone in the room noticing.

The rule-setting position is now built. The legitimacy loop has been running long enough that removing the governance authority would cost more than accepting it, and no within-system competitor can replicate what took years of participant ratification to accumulate and build. The rules govern the system. But governance at the level of rules is not the same as governance at the level of individual participants.

The architecture defines what is permitted. It cannot, by itself, tell you who has honoured it and who has not. Who has performed and who has defaulted. Whose history of interactions makes them trustworthy within the rules and whose does not. That record has to be built interaction by interaction, participant by participant, and building it requires a different sacrifice than the one that built the rule architecture itself. The next chapter asks what that sacrifice is.

SHARE THIS WITH SOMEONE?

I used to think competitive advantage was about being better within the rules. It took me a long time to see that the rules themselves are the prize, and that every rule structure we treat as given was built by someone who accepted a governance obligation their competitors refused.

Toussaint Louverture restored plantation labour and made trade agreements with slaveholders, and those moves look like betrayal until you understand that he was embedding governance institutions so deeply that Napoleon required betraying a flag of truce to remove him, and even that didn't stop the revolution.

Dee Hock was a vice president at a regional bank with no mandate and no equity stake, and he designed a payment network in which no bank, including the bank whose profitable franchise was the foundation of the entire system, would hold complete control.

Each bank that joined deepened the network's legitimacy. Each acceptance made the next acceptance more valuable. The Visa network eventually surpassed every competitor without the entity that built it owning any of the commercial upside. Edward Lloyd never underwrote a policy. Michelin never ran a restaurant, but governments now pay Michelin to extend its authority over their national culinary landscape.

The system anti-gambit competes for a share of what the rules permit. The Rule Architecture Gambit builds the position that determines what the rules permit. The mechanism is always the same: accept the governance obligation your competitors refuse, hold it through the period when it generates nothing, and watch each new participant who accepts governance deepen the legitimacy that enables higher-value rules.

The question isn't how to win within the existing structure. It's how to build a new structure, when the rule-setting throne is vacant.

GAMBIT EIGHT

TRUSTED NETWORK: VERIFIED THRESHOLD

Trusted Network: Verified Threshold

Lübeck, 1360. The Kontor counting house smells of greasy and acrid tallow smoke, as well as rotting fish brine and fermenting grain. The ledger open on the table is thicker than a Bible and bound in calfskin, worn smooth at the corners from decades of continuous use. Each entry notes a name, a city, a commodity, a date, a counterparty, and, in the rightmost column, in a cramped hand that varies because different clerks made different entries across different years, a settlement outcome: paid in full, delayed, settled with interest, disputed, arbitrated at Bruges, defaulted, member expelled, assets seized, and more.

The merchant consulting it this morning is deciding whether to extend credit to a man he has never met, for a shipment of Flemish cloth that will travel three weeks by sea before arriving at a Reval warehouse, where it will be held against a promissory note drawn on a Hamburg bank that the merchant also has never visited. Just this single transaction requires trusting four strangers in four cities across a thousand miles of the North Sea and Baltic coasts, with no legal enforcement mechanism operating simultaneously across all four jurisdictions, no common law, no shared sovereign, and no way to verify any of it in real time.

After a rigorous review, the merchant finally extends the credit. He is not naïve, because the man in question has a positive entry in the ledger and can therefore be trusted.

The Hanseatic League, the loose confederation of merchant cities and trading houses that controlled Baltic and North Sea commerce from roughly 1250 to 1650, is often remembered, if at all, as an early experiment in free trade or by some as a medieval forerunner to the European Union. Both descriptions are technically partly accurate, but both also miss the key structural mechanism entirely.

The Hanseatic League was much more than just a trade agreement. It was effectively an information architecture: a four-century-old trusted network based on a decentralized record of who had traded with whom, under what terms, and whether they had performed as contractually required.

The system worked like this. A merchant who wished to trade under the league's protections, with access to the Kontors, the trading posts in London, Bruges, Bergen, and Novgorod, preferential tariffs, a legal standing in Hanseatic courts, and protection from piracy through the League's naval enforcement, had to be a member in good standing of a member city's merchant guild. Membership required a verified reputation: references, a track record, and capital guarantees. Once admitted, every transaction was logged. Not by the merchant himself, but by various counterparties, by the Kontor clerks, or by guild officials in the respective city. The ledger was collective, distributed, and cross-referenced by cities that had no formal political reason to coordinate.

A Hamburg merchant's record in Lübeck's books was confirmed by entries in Danzig's books made by completely independent parties. A Lübeck merchant's record in Bruges was confirmed by records in Riga made years earlier by men who had never met the Bruges counterparties. The redundancy was the verification. Nobody could thus inflate their own record. Nobody could erase a default. The only way to build a good ledger entry was to perform repeatedly, with trust, across different counterparties, in different cities, over many years.

The Novgorod Kontor is proof of what this system uniquely achieved. Novgorod, in what is now north-western Russia, was the eastern terminus of the Baltic trade: the source of furs, wax, and amber that flowed west in exchange for cloth, metalwork, and salt. Hanseatic merchants operating in Novgorod were inside a hostile jurisdiction with no legal protections whatsoever. The Grand Prince could seize their goods, imprison them, cancel their privileges, and expel them entirely, and he did so periodically. In many ways, the only protection a Hanseatic merchant in Novgorod had was his collective identity as a Hanseatic merchant.

This identity was a sign of credible in Novgorod precisely because it was verified everywhere else. The Prince knew that Hanseatic merchants had trusted and verified reputations to protect, that their access to the entire Baltic network depended on their standing in the collective record, and that the collective record would document any Hanseatic betrayal of a Russian trading partner just as accurately as it documented any Russian betrayal of a Hanseatic one. The mutual verification created a deterrence structure that worked across jurisdictional boundaries because it did not depend on any single jurisdiction's enforcement.

The merchant in Lübeck closes the ledger and issues the credit note. He has no idea that what he is consulting is a structural condition of a system gambit, several centuries in the making. He knows it works. The conventional historical explanation of the Hanseatic League is justified by commercial geography. Control the key ports of Lübeck, Hamburg, Bruges, Bergen, Danzig, and in effect, you control the flows. The geographic monopoly was, it can be argued, the ultimate moat. The commercial success was then the consequence of that monopoly.

This reading of the Hanseatic League explains why the League existed in those key cities. Still, it does not explain why it lasted four centuries while everything else around it in Europe changed dramatically every few years. The core mechanism was more sophisticated than geography and seeing what it actually requires seeing the error most network builders make today.

Many investor-operators who build networks run same-side deepening: more buyers in a marketplace with buyers, more drivers on a platform with drivers, more merchants of the type already present. The number of headline participants continues to grow, and everyone from the board to the investors is happy. This is not the structural condition, because same-side growth produces diminishing returns per participant. Each additional participant of the same type adds marginally less than the one before. The network grows, but the value per participant does not compound.

The actual network effect is cross-side. Each new participant type that is complementary to the existing base generates superlinear value for every participant already present, not more of what was there, but a qualitatively different kind of value that neither side could produce without the other. More sellers make a platform more valuable to buyers in a way that is categorically different from more buyers making it marginally better for other buyers. One is the structural condition. The other is the system anti-gambit.

They look identical from a total participant count dashboard, and that is the trap. The Hanseatic League's competitors were running the system's anti-gambit and optimizing within it. The Italian city-states built extraordinarily trusted networks of merchants with sophisticated credit facilities. The Hanseatic League built something different. And the difference only became visible when it was already irreversible.

In That Meeting

The competitive pressure this chapter addresses creates a choice that most strategy sessions never really discuss. One competitor is growing much faster because it relaxed verification requirements six months ago, and their monthly active user count is accelerating. Someone, either the CFO or an investor representative, asks the following question: are the verification standards too strict, given where the market is moving?

On the other end of the table sits the entrepreneur–operator who has spent five years building the trusted verification infrastructure: completion rates are strong, repeat transaction volume is climbing, and, most importantly, fraud incidents are minimal. But the number of network participants is not growing too fast. The network effect threshold has not yet been reached, and everyone else in the room thinks it's time to cut corners to achieve that target.

The room is obsessed with reaching the network effects threshold. Two key loops run in the background: one that ensures quality by focusing on verification standards that build trust, and the other that ensures quantity by focusing on participant diversity to produce the liquidity that drives the platform's growth. Neither loop has crossed the threshold at which its output feeds the other loop's input in a way that becomes self-sustaining.

The corrective loop is running as the verification record builds trust. Still, without sufficient participant diversity, it is not yet producing cross-side value sufficient to justify the high cost of verification and infrastructure. The amplifying loop is also running, as participant diversity is growing slowly, but without sufficient verification depth, adverse selection could degrade match quality below what a verification loop enforces. Both of these investments are substantial, and to the hasty system-anti-gambit investor-operator, they both look like short-term underperformance.

The rational response is to commit to one side. This is not irrational. Single-sided deepening yields a higher total participant count within a quarter. The growth choice restores the headline total participant count to the trendline. But that short-term tweak has deep, long-term consequences, as it effectively traps the business in the system's anti-gambit.

The metrics that reveal whether the structural condition is building are not participant count or completion rate in isolation. They are whether the value per new verified participant of a complementary type is increasing, and whether match quality is increasing at the same time. If both trajectories are positive simultaneously, the network effects threshold is approaching faster. If one is improving at the expense of the other, the network operator is optimizing a trade-off, rather than growing to transcend it.

The pre-network-effects-threshold period always seems like underperformance. The correct response to short-term underperformance is to kill the underperforming investment. That is the trust network system anti-gambit trap.

SACRIFICE	STRUCTURAL CONDITION	COMPOUNDING LOGIC
The liquidity-reliability trade-off: choosing either verification depth or network scale, never both simultaneously. The management logic is rational and reinforced from both directions: investors enforce scale-axis logic, quality operators enforce verification-axis logic. Committing to one axis restores current-period metrics. Attempting both simultaneously satisfies neither benchmark during the investment period and looks, in every current measurement frame, like a failure to commit.	A verified cross-side value architecture where two loops run simultaneously: a corrective loop (verification infrastructure that records who participated and what quality they delivered, reducing adverse selection with each cycle) and an amplifying loop (cross-side network structure where each new complementary participant type generates super linear value for all existing participants). The structural condition is the product of both loops running together across the same participant base: not a large network, not a trusted network, but specifically a trusted large network that neither loop produces alone.	Each new verified participant raises expected match quality for all existing participants (corrective loop) while generating super linear cross-side value through complementarity (amplifying loop). Both loops compound simultaneously: return per verified match increases as verification history deepens; value per new verified participant increases as network density grows. The product widens every period without proportional additional investment. A late entrant cannot replicate the position by purchasing scale or building verification independently, because both loops must have run together across the same participant base from below the critical threshold. Five years of verified interactions at network scale cannot be bought. They can only be run.

The Mechanism

The sacrifice the trusted network gambit requires is this: forgoing the short-term growth that comes from deepening the participant type already present, at exactly the moment when a competitor who has dropped verification standards is accelerating their growth. The sacrifice is real because the investor reporting deck will show slower participant count, higher onboarding costs, and worse headline metrics during the dual-investment period. People will be unhappy, pressure will be applied to cut corners, and that is why it is a genuine and painful sacrifice.

What the sacrifice purchases is a unique structural condition: a participant base in which verified cross-side complementarity generates super linear interaction value. The product of a corrective loop and an amplifying loop running simultaneously across the same participants. The corrective loop records performance, detects quality failures, and raises the reliability of every future match. The amplifying loop expands participant type diversity, so that each new complementary participant generates value for every existing participant of a different type. Each loop complements and reinforces the other in ways neither can achieve alone.

The compounding logic works like this: verification depth makes each new complementary participant's decision to join less risky, attracting more complementary types, generating more cross-side transactions, generating more verification entries, deepening the record further, and making the next participant's decision even less risky.' Each cycle produces the input that makes the next cycle more productive without equivalent additional investment. The moat this builds cannot be breached by a competitor that allocates more capital, because five years of simultaneous loop operation cannot be bought; it can only be run and built.

To see why both loops are necessary, start by running the amplifying loop without the corrective loop.

The Counts of Champagne, ruling a landlocked county in north-eastern France between around 1150 and 1285, had nothing to trade. Champagne produced no significant export commodity. Its geographic position between the cloth-producing regions of Flanders to the north and the Italian city-states to the south gave it proximity to two trading hubs that needed each other and had no reliable convergence point.

Every other feudal lord in Europe with comparable geography ran the locally optimal management logic: extract rents from any commercial concentration that emerged, grant privileges to favoured guilds, and heavily tax the merchants passing through.

The Counts of Champagne did the opposite. They issued generalized guarantees to all merchants, nationalities, guilds, and religions. They built a dedicated fair police force, operated more than four tiers of public courts, regulated weights and measures, and extended protection beyond their own territory at direct political cost.

When a French nobleman robbed moneychangers in Vézelay en route to the Provins fair in 1148, Count Thibault II wrote to the regent of France demanding compensation, effectively spending his political capital to secure redress for people who were not his subjects for wrongs he had not committed.

The management logic antagonism here is evident. The extractive feudal logic and the participant-diversity logic are mutually exclusive within the same governance structure. Every guild privilege granted would have excluded non-guild members. Every differential tax would have reduced one side's incentive to attend. Every extracted rent would have reduced the surplus available for cross-side transactions. The sacrifice was a short-term extraction, forgone for participant diversity, that had not yet arrived.

- The architecture that emerged had three interlocking participant types:
- Northern merchants brought cloth, wool, and furs that southern Europe needed;
- Southern merchants brought spices, silk, and luxury goods that northern Europe needed.
- Italian bankers and money changers provided bills of exchange, credit, and settlement services that enabled large-scale transactions for both parties.

Each new southern merchant made every northern merchant's position more valuable. Each new banker made clearing cheaper for both sides, which made the journey worth it for more merchants of both types. By the mid-thirteenth century, a continuous six-fair cycle spanning the calendar year had emerged. Contracts across medieval European commerce were worded to expire "at the next Champagne fair". The Counts had built the settlement infrastructure for all of northern Europe's trade, successfully executing the trusted network system gambit.

Then the French crown inherited Champagne in 1285 and replaced generalized institutional services with individual privileges granted to specific merchant communities to serve short-term royal policy. The other merchants moved to Bruges, Antwerp, and Lyon instead. The compounding loop that had taken 130 years to build unwound within two decades.

The mechanism that resulted in the collapse was interestingly not external competition as one might suppose. It was a management logic reversal. The extractive logic and the participant-diversity logic cannot coexist within the same governance structure. The moment the operator prioritizes short-term extraction over maintaining participant diversity, cross-side amplification begins to degrade. The participant type most subject to extraction reduces engagement. The complementary type finds the platform less valuable without them. The network density loop begins to reverse.

This is the structural basis of what Cory Doctorow calls enshittification. Every contemporary platform that has degraded from its peak compounding position has done so by reverting to extractive management logic. Once cross-side participants have been locked in, the platform begins to worsen and enshittify the experience for all sides simultaneously, thereby extracting more from all sides while keeping them locked in. It is the structural consequence of the two antagonistic logics sharing the same locus of decision-making.

The Champagne Fairs ran the amplifying loop without the corrective loop. That is why they compounded for 130 years and collapsed within just a few years. Cross-side participant diversity yielded a super-linear value. Without a verification infrastructure, without a distributed record of who had performed and who had defaulted, the network's trust depended entirely on the governance remaining neutral. When the governance changed, there was nothing structural to hold the network together. The condition dissolved rapidly due to political changes. The Hanseatic League ran both loops simultaneously. This is why it lasted four centuries.

The corrective loop, the distributed, connected but independent Hanseatic ledgers, made the amplifying loop durable. A merchant's verified record was visible to every other Hanseatic merchant in every other city. The verification did not depend on any single political authority remaining neutral. It was distributed across cities that had no other reason to coordinate, cross-referenced against entries made by independent parties, and self-correcting: a merchant who defaulted lost standing in every city simultaneously, not just where the default occurred. The corrective loop was the governance architecture that made the amplifying loop safe to run across jurisdictions where no single sovereign could enforce it.

The product of both loops running together is not the sum of their separate contributions. The corrective loop improves the quality of every cross-side match produced by the amplifying loop. The amplifying loop raises the number and variety of complementary participants whose presence the corrective loop can improve. More verified merchant types meant more cross-side transactions; more transactions meant more ledger entries; more entries meant a more precise trust signal; a more precise trust signal made each new participant's decision to join less risky, which attracted more participant types, which generated more transactions. Each cycle compounded both dimensions simultaneously.

Warren Buffett, along with his long-time business partner Charlie Munger, built the same architecture across 60 years. Berkshire Hathaway's annual shareholder meeting began with only 12 attendees in 1965. Six decades later, it draws well over 40,000 people to Omaha each spring. The growth in attendance is the visible output of the amplifying loop. Less visible is the corrective loop that made it durable.

The corrective loop was designed at inception through a deliberate participant filter. "We never sought out professional investors to join our partnerships. Among all my partners, I never had a single institution, I never wanted an institution," Buffett stated at the 2025 annual meeting.

This was in effect a governance decision about what the verification record needed to be. The institutional investor optimizes for quarterly performance relative to the benchmark, has fiduciary obligations that may require selling in adverse market conditions, and generates precisely the kind of short-term noise that destroys trust-building over long cycles. Excluding institutions at entry was a decision to build a participant base whose behaviour of holding through downturns, treating shares as long-term ownership stakes, and engaging with the company's reasoning rather than its short-term price, would create co-ownership depth rather than the typical Wall Street transactional frequency.

In that sense, the annual letter is the corrective loop's primary instrument. Every year, Buffett writes directly to shareholders—not Wall Street analysts, not institutions, not the financial press—explaining what happened, why it happened, and most importantly, what mistakes were made. Each entry is cross-checkable against subsequent outcomes, self-incriminating when wrong, and therefore credible in a way no self-serving short-term–minded corporate communication can be.

After 60 years of entries, the record is the most extensive verified management track record in public markets. It is not a marketing document. It is a distributed ledger of managerial performance and reasoning, in some ways structurally analogous to the Hanseatic ledgers, running at an annual frequency rather than per transaction.

The amplifying loop runs through the meeting itself. A long-term Berkshire shareholder who has attended for 20 years has built a verified social and intellectual network that no new entrant can replicate by simply purchasing shares. Guy Spier's annual VALUExBRK is a highlight.

The meeting connects shareholders with Berkshire's subsidiary business managers, potential acquisition targets, and an investing culture that treats Omaha almost like an annual pilgrimage. Each cross-side interaction generates the same kind of value that the Champagne Fairs generated between cloth merchants and spice merchants: something neither side could produce without the co-presence of the other.

The outcome is a shareholder base that is structurally and fundamentally different from any other company in public markets. Berkshire shareholders do not sell when the market drops. They provide stable capital that allows long-term investments that competitors with more transactional shareholder bases cannot make. The trusted network enables the investment strategy. The investment strategy generates the performance. The performance deepens the trusted network. Each cycle compounds both dimensions simultaneously.

For a younger demographic, Airbnb proves the same mechanism in a pure marketplace context. The two-directional review system is the corrective loop: it records the behaviour of both guests and hosts, detects quality deviations, and feeds that information back into the matching architecture so higher-verified participants attract better counterparties and lower-verified participants face higher friction.

The two-sided host–guest network is the amplifying loop: each new verified host makes the platform more valuable to guests; each new verified guest makes the platform more valuable to hosts; and because both sides are verified, the option value compounds rather than erodes through adverse selection. A host with 200 verified reviews across 15 countries is not just more reliable than a host with two reviews. They are a qualitatively different type of participant. Their presence generates cross-side value that compounds the entire network in ways an unverified host of equivalent quality cannot. Below a certain verification depth, the participant is treated as another node. Above it, they generate value that self-reinforces across the entire system.

The trusted network system gambit requires building both loops simultaneously, sacrificing the immediate returns of each. A late entrant cannot replicate this position by purchasing scale, because scale without simultaneous verification results in failure. And of course, scale without verification is always faster to build. The sacrifice is the dual-investment period during which both loops are running, and neither produces the metrics required to satisfy a single-sided measurement frame. Compounding is the structural condition that arises when the product of both loops exceeds the threshold.

> ***Most operators are running the system anti-gambit. Same-side deepening looks like a network effect and generates diminishing returns per participant. The structural condition is different: verification makes cross-side scale safe to build; cross-side scale makes verification compound. Neither produces the position alone. Neither can be built sequentially. The sacrifice is the dual-investment period when both loops are running and neither looks like it's working. That period is not underperformance. It is the gambit.***

The Failure of Extraction

The failure mode usually occurs precisely at the moment the gambit begins to compound. As the trusted network system gambit crosses the network effects threshold, the verification infrastructure that was holding quality stable as the network grew comes under pressure from the network's own success.

The Champagne Fairs prove this historically: a loop that took 130 years to build unwound within a few short years when the governance logic that built it suddenly reverted. The French crown, which inherited Champagne in 1285, did not commit a moral error. It made the locally optimal management logic choice: particularized privilege grants generate more current-period political capital than generalized institutional services do. Every single choice was rational. The aggregate structural consequence was catastrophic and irreversible.

This is enshittification in action. Not necessarily a moral failing, but a management logic reversion: the inevitable consequence of an investor–operator who has built a cross-side verified network, gradually shifting back towards extractive logic once the participant base is large enough to extract from.

The reversion looks like small, rational optimizations: charge higher fees to the participant type that most needs the platform; prioritize those who pay for visibility; slightly reduce verification standards to increase onboarding speed. Each choice improves current-period metrics. Each choice degrades the cross-side amplification that made both participant types valuable.

Eventually, the participant type most subject to extraction reduces engagement. The complementary type finds the platform less valuable without them. The network density loop begins to reverse. The structural condition that took years to build degrades faster than it was built, because compounding runs downward as readily as it runs upwards.

A second failure mode is verification degradation under the pressure of the amplifying loop. Growing participant counts mean more records to maintain, more edge cases to adjudicate, and more sophisticated actors who have studied the verification system and learned to game its inputs. The corrective loop's institutional capacity grows linearly. The number of participants in the amplifying loop grows super linearly. At some scale, the corrective loop falls behind, verification quality degrades, and the trust record begins to mean less per interaction than it did when the network was smaller. An algorithm that processes hundreds of data points to generate a trust score is not doing what a community that has built a reputation network over years of actual interaction does. The score looks like the record, but it is not.

The most dangerous failure mode is governance capture. The corrective loop requires someone to decide what counts as a quality failure, what threshold triggers exclusion, and what standards the verification record is measuring. Whoever controls the definition of "verified" controls the corrective loop, and therefore the entry conditions for the amplifying loop that runs on top of it. This saga played out in front of everyone on Twitter-to-X.

In a small verified network, this governance is tractable. At scale, it becomes a problem of power concentration and a juicy target for extraction. The Hanseatic League's governance failures in its final century were precisely this: which cities had the authority to admit members, who could override a Kontor's quality judgement, and how the collective record adjudicated disputes between members of different guilds with different local standards. The corrective loop did not fail. The amplifying loop's interests captured the governance by the corrective loop.

Berkshire's version of this complication is straightforward. The annual letter and the meeting maintain their corrective loop integrity precisely because Buffett writes the letter himself, in his own voice, without intermediation. The complication Berkshire now faces, which Greg Abel has explicitly acknowledged, is whether verification governance can be maintained institutionally once the person who generated it is no longer the primary protagonist.

The complication does not invalidate the system gambit. Instead, it defines its second-order requirement: the governance of the verification standard must be designed as a separate, protected layer that the amplifying loop's growth pressure cannot directly reach.

The participant diversity logic and the extractive logic must be kept structurally separated in the governance architecture, because the moment they share the same decision-making locus, locally rational choices begin to align towards the extractive management logic, from which no trusted network system has ever recovered.

Think, Share, Discuss

In any room where a decision is being made about network growth, marketplace design, or trust infrastructure investment, two questions change the conversation:

> ***"Is the growth investment going into a complementary participant type whose co-presence generates cross-side super linear value?"***
>
> ***And the most important question:***
>
> ***"Is the governance that protects the verification standard structurally separated from the governance that measures participant count?"***

The first one cannot be answered by someone who thinks same-side deepening and cross-side amplification are the same thing. The second one cannot be answered by someone who treats verification quality as an operational cost rather than a governance architecture question.

If the platform is growing participants of the type it already has and calling it a network effect, the system anti-gambit is running in full swing. If the platform is growing complementary participant types, but the verification standard and the extraction incentive share the same decision-making body, the system gambit is hurtling towards its complication.

The trusted network gambit ends with a question its own success creates: who governs the verification standard once the network is large enough to make that standard worth capturing?

SHARE THIS WITH SOMEONE?

Most networks hit a ceiling they can't explain, and the explanation is not about trust or network effects in isolation.

The thing most operators are calling a network effect is same-side deepening: more participants of the type already present, generating diminishing returns per participant. The structural condition is different.

Verification makes cross-side scale safe to build and cross-side scale makes verification compound. Importantly, neither produces the position alone, and neither can be built sequentially, because a late entrant who builds scale first produces guaranteed failure, and a late entrant who builds verification first produces a small network that cannot instantly generate super-linear cross-side value.

The Counts of Champagne ran the amplifying loop for 130 years and it collapsed within a few years when the governance reverted.

The Hanseatic League ran both loops for four centuries because the distributed, independent but interconnected ledgers held the amplifying loop together, despite any single sovereign's political will.

Every marketplace trade of verification for growth to hit a headline metric is foreclosing the only structural position that competitors cannot replicate later regardless of investment.

CONCLUSION

THE AI IMPACT

Conclusion: The AI Impact

All eight system gambits in this book share one structural similarity: abandoning a management logic that is still working, because this current management logic and system is blocking access to the new system with a self-reinforcing feedback loop that results in compounding value. Yi Sun-sin abandoned territorial defence to deny supply lines. Toyota abandoned individual line speed to close the kanban loop. Morris Chang abandoned chip design to build the foundry interface. In each case, the new and old logic could not coexist within the same operating frame, and the structural impossibility of running both management logics simultaneously was the source of the moat as the compounding of value.

AI is the first major commercial technology in modern memory that requires no such antagonism to deploy. It gets bolted onto whichever paradigm is currently running. An industrial business uses it to optimize its processes more efficiently than before. A digital business uses it to validate use cases faster than before. A platform business uses it to increase interactions more effortlessly.

None of this AI adoption forces the investor–operator to abandon the prevailing management logic. And hence none of this can produce a compounding position, because the structural condition this book has identified for compounding requires exactly the antagonism that AI adoption does not impose. AI adoption, at best, yields commoditized within-paradigm improvements that approach zero excess return as adoption diffuses across an industry.

The first-order consequence is by now widely felt and evident. Most of the AI adoption currently being built and funded will produce neither structural asymmetric advantage nor compounding returns, because the same efficiency gains they promise is available to every competitor with a credit card and API key.

The second-order consequence matters more for the ambitious investor–operator reading this book. AI does not eliminate compounding when it commoditizes within-paradigm optimization across the economy. It concentrates it rapidly at exactly the points AI cannot reach, and the eight system gambits this book has covered correspond, one to one, to those points. Each system gambit, identifies a structural condition that AI cannot create.

The first big unlock is recognizing the paradigm shift itself. Value comes from the willingness to abandon metrics calibrated to the current paradigm's binding constraint before the market notices the constraint has moved. Oda Nobunaga did not win because he adopted the Tanegashima gun faster than rival warlords. He won because he was willing to abandon the samurai paradigm's individual-valour benchmarks. AI does not produce this willingness because AI is trained on data generated by the current paradigm.

The second is constraint-level signal placement, whose value comes from physical or institutional proximity to the binding bottleneck. Toyota's Andon cord and kanban placed signals at the constraint and at the constraint's clock speed, and GM's failure to replicate the system was not a failure of the visible practices but of the receiving system and architecture that would have made the signal actionable. AI adoption that aggregates several layers above the core constraint produces confident readings of an open loop, which is worse than producing nothing at all, because the confidence crowds out the discomfort that would have driven correction if the loop were closed at the core constraint.

The third is the hard-to-vary causal model, whose value lies in its structural inability to accommodate observations without breaking. Brahe's measurements were valuable because their precision was intolerant of any cosmological theory that was not empirically true, and Kepler's elliptical orbits were powerful because altering any component would break the entire predictive structure. AI is constitutionally the opposite. AI optimizes to fit observed data, meaning its models accommodate observations rather than rejecting them, and most operators now use AI as a substitute for ever having to commit to a falsifiable explanation of why their constraint the way it does.

The fourth is the cross-paradigm coupling architecture, whose value comes from a routing layer that closes loops between paradigms with structurally antagonistic management logics. Amazon's industrial-digital-platform coupling runs through Prime, FBA and AWS, because the routing between components allows each paradigm's output to become the input that improves the next paradigm's cycle, while preserving each paradigm's distinct discipline. AI does not build this kind coupling. It optimizes within whichever paradigm it is adopted in, and the institutional discipline required to route outputs rigorously across paradigm boundaries is governance work, not AI model work.

The fifth is causal decentralization, whose value lies in distributed decision-makers running their own decision cycles faster than the environment's clock speed, each based on the same causal model. Malik Ambar's bargigiri operated a decentralized decision cycle embedded within the Mughal decision cycle, and the Mughal command structure could not match that clock speed. Most AI deployments centralize judgement in the model layer and propagate it back through dashboards, which reflects an architecture of slow, centralized decision-making rather than fast, distributed decision-making.

The sixth is the stable interface, whose value lies in the specification not changing. ARM's 35 years of neutrality and TSMC's foundry pledge are great examples of this. AI raises the value of stable interfaces rather than lowering it, because the rate of model change renders anything tightly coupled to a specific model architecture obsolete within 12 to 18 months.

The seventh is the rule-setting position, whose value comes from accepted governance obligation rather than from technical capability. Visa's authority is based on its capability to govern across a global network of banks, merchants and individuals. AI does not automatically generate legitimacy.

The thrones currently vacant will be occupied by operators whose key capability is governance discipline rather than model capability.

The eighth is the verified interaction history, whose value derives from the time that actually elapsed during verification. The Hanseatic ledger could not be retroactively built in 1450 by any merchant, irrespective of their wealth, because the entries had to have been made in 1300, 1325, and 1370 by independent parties. AI enhances rather than weakens this property. As synthetic identity and synthetic transaction patterns proliferate, verified history becomes the scarce input AI itself cannot produce, and the operators who began accumulating it five or ten years ago at visible cost to growth metrics are already in a structurally different system from late entrants funding scale on unverified counts.

SHARE THIS WITH SOMEONE?

The structural asymmetric advantages that survive AI commoditization are the ones AI cannot generate: paradigm judgement, constraint-level signal placement, hard-to-vary causal models, cross-paradigm coupling, distributed decision authority, stable specifications, ratified governance obligation, and trusted network history.

These eight system gambits are where the next decades of compounding will concentrate. The rest will increasingly lose value or get commoditized.

AI is not the system gambit. AI is the new force that makes every system anti-gambit less valuable, faster, than at any prior point in business history.

The system gambit still requires a sacrifice. What AI has done is exploded the cost of refusing the system gambit.

Don't Stop Compounding Now!

Congratulations on reading *The System Gambit*!

I'm truly honoured to have you as a reader and I'm grateful for the time and energy you invested to read this book.

Putting all relevant materials and details in the book would have made it unwieldy and unreadable. So I have curated several resources for you to leverage right after reading this book. As the author, my goal is to show my gratitude to you for having engaged deeply with *The System Gambit*, and to give you useful resources to allow you to leverage system gambits in your business, work, career and life.

Supporting Materials and Worksheets

Get the most updated free supporting materials, worksheets and latest insights about *The System Gambit* by signing up at **thesystemgambit.substack.com**

Bonus Chapter: The Emerging AI Paradigm

If you enjoyed *The System Gambit*, I'd be delighted if you could write a review on Amazon to help like-minded people discover the book more easily.

To thank you for taking the time to do so, I'd love to give you exclusive access to the most up to date version of a special bonus chapter about The Emerging AI Paradigm, and its implications to business, technology, value creation and compounding.

Please send a link to your review to **team@thesystemgambit.com** to get special access.

Invite Ritavan for a Keynote or Workshop

The System Gambit's author Ritavan accepts a handful of invitations to give keynotes or conduct workshops about how to execute *The System Gambit* for your business.

To invite Ritavan to speak, find all relevant details on **ritavan.com** and send an email to **team@thesystemgambit.com**

APPENDIX

COMMON MISUNDERSTANDINGS

Appendix: Common Misunderstandings

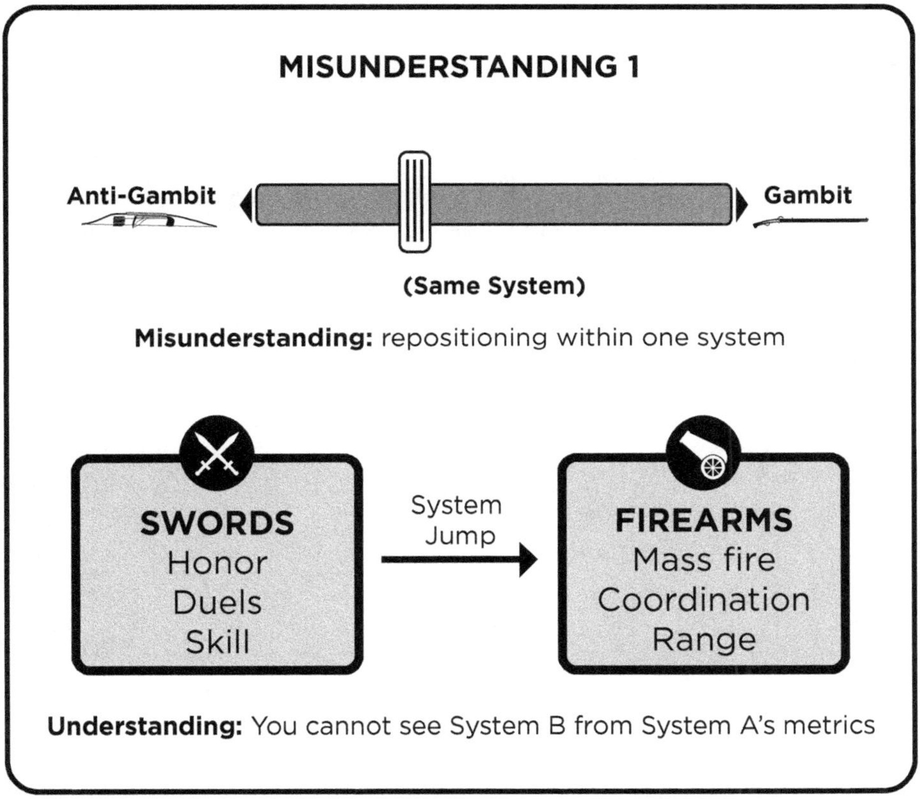

The system anti-gambit and the system gambit are not properties of the same system.

The formulation is sometimes misinterpreted to suggest that the system anti-gambit and the system gambit are two properties of the same system, as if the system gambit were a reallocation from one dimension to another within a single system. This is a common misunderstanding. The system anti-gambit is a position within the current system, defined by that system's metrics, management norms, and benchmark structures. The system gambit is a structural feature of another system, one that does not yet fully exist when the sacrifice is made, or that exists but is invisible to the current system's benchmarks.

Nobunaga's generals were not operating within the prevailing samurai warfare paradigm. Coordinated mass firepower was not a different metric in that system. It was an entirely different system of warfare, with different units of competitive advantage, different management logic, and a different causal structure. The system gambit was not an optimization choice within existing warfare. It was a deliberate system crossing into a new system altogether.

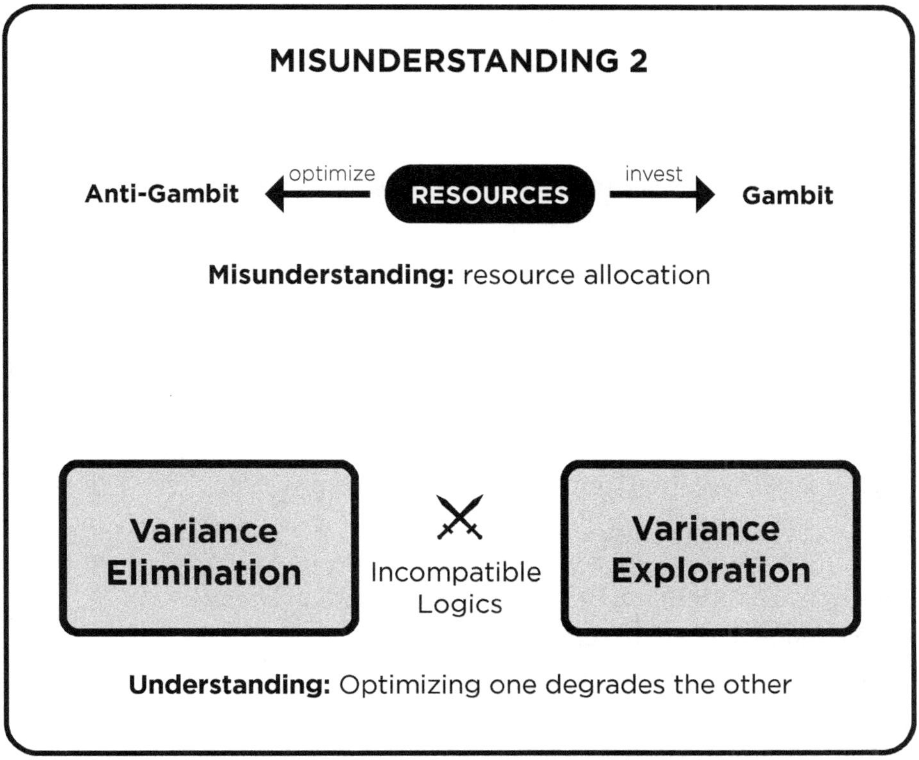

The sacrifice is a system crossing, not a resource reallocation. Describing the sacrifice as "reducing performance on the system anti-gambit to free resources for the system gambit" makes it sound like a portfolio reallocation decision: spend less here, invest more there. The deeper structure is different. The management logic required to optimize the anti-gambit is structurally incompatible with that required to build the gambit. They are not just different priorities. They actively destroy each other.

Variance elimination is the correct management logic for industrial process optimization. Variance exploration is the correct management logic for digital use case validation. You cannot operate both simultaneously. The sacrifice of the system anti-gambit is not a resource decision. It is the abandonment of a management logic that prevents the gambit from existing.

Recommended Reading

Thinking in Systems: A Primer
by Donella Meadows

The Education Of A Value Investor: My Transformative Quest For Wealth, Wisdom, And Enlightenment
by Guy Spier

Impact Banker by Alexander Hoare

Hate the Game: Economic Cheat Codes for Life, Love, and Work
by Daryl Fairweather

Reshuffle: Who Wins When AI Restacks the Knowledge Economy
by Sangeet Paul Choudary

The Digital Phoenix Effect: How Legacy Companies Can Lead the Platform Revolution Without Burning Everything Down
by Daniel Trabucchi and Tommaso Buganza

Just Evil Enough: The Subversive Marketing Handbook
by Alistair Croll and Emily Ross

Lean Analytics: Use Data to Build a Better Startup Faster
by Alistair Croll and Ben Yoskovitz

Richer, Wiser, Happier
by William Green

The Origins of Efficiency
by Brian Potter

Enshittification
by Cory Doctorow

RECOMMENDED READING

FOCUS: The ASML Way
by Marc Hijink

BREAKPOINT: The Crisis of the Middle Class and the Future of Work
by Saurabh Mukherjea, et al

The Nutmeg's Curse
by Amitav Ghosh

Apple in China: The Capture of the World's Greatest Company
by Patrick McGee

Atypical: Five Strategy Rules for a New World
by Prateek Raj

Higher Ground: How Business Can Do the Right Thing in a Turbulent World
by Alison Taylor

The Unseen Leader: How History Can Help Us Rethink Leadership
by Martin Gutmann

The Lean Startup
by Eric Ries

The Business of Platforms: Strategy in the Age of Digital Competition, Innovation, and Power
by Annabelle Gawer, David B. Yoffie, and Michael A. Cusumano

The Decision Factory: A Novel about Decisions Under Uncertainty
by John Brandon Elam and Adam David DeJans Jr.

Acknowledgements

I'd like to thank my cover and interior designer Mike Trent, who has been a constant pillar of support, encouragement and motivation during the writing of this book. He has been an excellent and calming brainstorming partner, and I cannot think of ever writing a book without him by my side. I'd also like to thank my copyeditor Vidisha Ghosh for helping with correcting, polishing and formatting the text. And while we're at it, thank you Lou Franco for introducing me to Mike and thank you Aurodeep Mukherjee for introducing me to Vidisha.

I would like to thank my early beta-readers and in particular Stefan Stoll, Ratul Ahmed, Shamik Biswas, Devarshi Das and Dora Simroth for reading the entire manuscript and sharing their feedback, as well as to Dustin Schafer, Hari Ramsamy, Dani Solà Lagares, . I'm grateful to Rahul Dharod for helping me craft a useful glossary from a reader's perspective. I'm honoured by all the time the brilliant people I deeply admire, who spent reading The System Gambit pre-launch and sharing their blurbs. Your names are already everywhere!

Last year after the launch of *Data Impact*, I'm grateful to all my readers and reviewers who told me they liked the book but that they were now hungry for more. They asked me to further expand on the "Leverage" step from my SLASOG framework.

I'm grateful to my friend and fellow author Lou Franco for nudging me to read Donella Meadows' classic on systems thinking in the early summer last year. Her book was on my reading list, but it is Lou's nudge that got me started and once I started, I couldn't stop thinking in systems. In that sense, this book is a small homage to the memory of Donella Meadows, for the inspiring work she left for us to cherish.

I'm grateful to Guy Spier for having inspired me by his book *The Education of a Value Investor*, his kind hand-written note, his invitation to this his podcast, and his nudge to get me started on my journey of hosting my own podcast Part-Maven Part-Maverick.

I'm grateful to the guests of my podcast, whose books stretched my horizons and deepened my knowledge. This book has many flashes of what I learned either directly or indirectly via the fantastic authors and operators who appeared on my podcast.

Finally, I'm grateful to my family and close friends, many of whom have no interest at all in my books and writings: they help my mad obsessive mind occasionally disconnect from continuously cogitating. And most importantly, I owe deep appreciation to my wife Moutoshi who admirably and to my utter amazement manages to successfully navigate the entire spectrum between being my greatest pillar of support in my darkest moments, as well as my most dismissive critic in my moments of vanity and hubris. I'm blessed to be with you.

Notes

The System Gambit

1. 'History of Admiral Yi', Yi Sun Sin World, https://www.yisunsinworld.com/history-of-admiral-yi
2. 'The Kobukson or Turtle Ship', War History, https://warhistory.org/article/the-kobukson-or-turtle-ship/
3. 'Yi-Sun-Shin', Encyclopaedia Britannica, https://www.britannica.com/biography/Yi-Sun-shin
4. 'Complementary Keys to Naval Victory', Naval History Magazine, https://www.usni.org/magazines/naval-history magazine/2009/august/complementary-keys-naval-victory
5. 'Understanding the Structure of the Panokseon, the Main Warship of the Joseon Navy', Journal of Military History (KCI), https://journal.kci.go.kr/imhc/archive/articleView?artiId=ART003219757
6. 'Tribute to Korea's greatest military hero Yi Sun-sin', Korea.net, https://www.korea.net/NewsFocus/HonoraryReporters/view?articleId=195238
7. 'This Admiral Never Lost a Single Vessel — And May Have Invented the Armored Ship', HistoryNet, https://www.historynet.com/yi-sun-sin/
8. 'Admiral Yi Sun-Shin, the Turtle Ships, and Modern Asian History', Asia in World History vol. 12, no. 1, https://www.asianstudies.org/publications/eaa/archives/admiral-yi-sun-shin-the-turtle-ships-and-modern-asian-history/
9. 'Turtle Ship', University of Hawai'i, https://www2.hawaii.edu/~sford/research/turtle/index.html
10. 'Jeolla in Imjin War', Gwangju News, https://gwangjunewsgic.com/features/jeolla-history/jeolla-in-yimjin/

NOTES

Goal Displacement: Paradigm Change

1. 'A Brief History of Japan's Daimyo Lords', Thought Co., https://www.thoughtco.com/a-brief-history-japans-daimyo-lords-195308
2. 'A Lesson on Worldly Wisdom', FS Blog, https://fs.blog/great-talks/a-lesson-on-worldly-wisdom/
3. 'Aichi Now – Spot Detail', Aichinow, https://aichinow.pref.aichi.jp/en/spots/detail/310/
4. 'Battle of Nagashino', Britannica, https://www.britannica.com/event/Battle-of-Nagashino
5. 'Battle of Sekigahara', National Park Service, https://www.nps.gov/articles/000/battle-of-sekigahara.htm
6. 'Charles Munger: The Cost-Cutting Phenomenon', The Acquirer's Multiple, https://acquirersmultiple.com/2023/08/charles-munger-the-cost-cutting-phenomenon/
7. 'Covid-19 Has Accelerated Digital Transformation, but May Have Made it Harder Not Easier', MIS Quarterly Executive, https://doi.org/10.17705/2msqe.00034
8. 'EP03: The History of Guns in Medieval Japan', Samurai Podcast, https://samuraipodcast.com/ep03-the-history-of-guns-in-medieval-japan
9. 'Europeans Begin Trade with Japan', Gamers Guide to Feudal Japan, https://www.ebsco.com/research-starters/history/europeans-begin-trade-japan
10. 'Firearms in Japan', War History, https://warhistory.org/article/firearms-in-japan
11. 'How the Battle of Okehazama Changed Japanese History', Sengoku Chronicles, https://sengokuchronicles.com/how-the-battle-of-okehazama-changed-japanese-history/
12. 'How Were Samurai Paid', Kyujutsu.co, https://kyujutsu.co.uk/knowledge/f/how-were-samurai-paid
13. 'Inside Mori Clan Armour – Fear, Function, and Samurai Legacy', BBC https://www.bbc.co.uk/programmes/p0mn8l4t
14. 'Japan in Chaos: Sengoku Period', Old Dominion University, http://odu.edu/sites/default/files/documents/ib-crisis-japan-in-chaos.pdf
15. 'Japan Up Magazine Article', Japan Up Magazine, https://japanupmagazine.com/archives/2335
16. 'Japan's New Way of War', War History, https://www.warhistoryonline.com/instant-articles/japans-new-way-of-war.html
17. 'Japan's Richest Domains in the Edo Period', Nippon, https://www.nippon.com/en/japan-data/h01683/

18. 'Japanese Civilization (Part 9) - A World Order Dominated by the Gun', Special Article,
http://jef.or.jp/journal/pdf/Specialartc0307.pdf

19. 'Japanese Tanegashima Musketry',
https://medium.com/@harunakahoshino/japanese-tanegashima-musketry-2e60b1726d48

20. 'Kokudaka', Japan Reference,
https://jref.com/articles/kokudaka.284/

21. 'Mori Family', Britannica,
https://www.britannica.com/topic/Mori-family

22. 'Mori Nagayoshi', Samurai History,
https://samuraihistoryculture.substack.com/p/mori-nagayoshi

23. 'Nippon.com Guide to Japan', Nippon,
https://www.nippon.com/en/guide-to-japan/gu900147/

24. 'Oda Nobuhide: The Tiger of Owari', Samurai History Culture,
https://samuraihistoryculture.substack.com/p/oda-nobuhide-the-tiger-of-owari

25. 'Oda Nobunaga and the Gunpowder Revolution in Japan', Medievalists,
https://www.medievalists.net/2021/04/oda-nobunaga-and-the-gunpowder-revolution-in-japan/

26. 'Oda Nobunaga Through a New Lens: Historians Are Overturning the Old Narrative', Japan Forward,
https://japan-forward.com/oda-nobunaga-through-a-new-lens-historians-are-overturning-the-old-narrative/

27. 'Oda Nobunaga: The Rise of One of Japan's Earliest Unifiers', Warfare History Network, 'Oda Nobunaga', EBSCO,
https://www.ebsco.com/research-starters/history/oda-nobunaga

28. 'Oda Nobunaga', World History,
https://www.worldhistory.org/Oda_Nobunaga/

29. 'Rice and History', Sumitomo,
https://www.sumitomo.gr.jp/english/history/s_history/rice/

30. 'Samurai Firearms', History Skills,
https://www.historyskills.com/classroom/year-8/samurai-firearms/?srsltid=AfmBOoor-BAMBiLU_FCyDmRJFcLu7sNUa335H4qiNW7slQY-g2EO7mLjB

31. 'Samurai Monetary System', Diffworlds,
https://www.diffworlds.com/samurai/monetary_system.htm

32. 'Sekigahara Battlefield Museum: Relive One of the Most Important Moments in Japan's History', Japan Today,
https://japantoday.com/category/features/travel/sekigahara-battlefield-museum-relive-one-of-the-most-important-moments-in-japan's-history

33. 'Sengoku Period', Britannica,
https://www.britannica.com/topic/Sengoku-period

34. 'Takeda Shingen', Britannica,
https://www.britannica.com/biography/Takeda-Shingen

NOTES

35. 'The impact of pikes and guns in Sengoku-Period Japan', Denison University,
https://digitalcommons.denison.edu/cgi/viewcontent.cgi?article=1032&context=studentscholarship

36. 'The Story of the Battle of Sekigahara', Nakasenodoway,
https://www.nakasendoway.com/the-story-of-the-battle-of-sekigahara/

37. 'The Three Great Spears of Japan', Samurai History Culture,
https://samuraihistoryculture.substack.com/p/the-three-great-spears-of-japan

38. 'The Three Unifiers of Sengoku Era Japan', Japan Society,
https://japansociety.org/news/the-three-unifiers-of-sengoku-era-japan/

39. 'Uesugi Family', Britannica,
https://www.britannica.com/topic/Uesugi-family

40. 'War and State Building in Medieval Japan – Instruments of Change, Organizational Technology and the Consolidation',
https://tconlan.scholar.princeton.edu/sites/g/files/toruqf3991/files/tconlan/files/war_and_state_building_in_medieval_japan_-_7._instruments_of_change_organizational_technology_and_the_consolidati._copy.pdf

41. 'Weapons', Kogakure,
https://www.kogakure.de/en/weapons/

42. George Sansom, *A History of Japan*, 1334–1615, 1961, Stanford University Press.

43. Stephen Turnbull, *War in Japan*: 1467–1615, 2002, Osprey Publishing.

44. Thomas Conlan, *Weapons and Fighting Techniques of the Samurai Warrior: 1200–1877 AD, 2022*, Amber Books Ltd.

Signal Quality: Core Bottleneck

1. '10 Things You May Not Know About the Battle of the Bulge', History Collection, https://historycollection.com/10-things-may-not-know-battle-bulge/
2. 'Anthony C. McAuliffe', Britannica, https://www.britannica.com/biography/Anthony-C-McAuliffe
3. 'Antoni van Leeuwenhoek', Brunel, https://www.brunel.net/en/blog/business-insights/antoni-van-leeuwenhoek
4. 'Antonie van Leeuwenhoek and the Discovery of Microorganisms', PubMed Central, https://pmc.ncbi.nlm.nih.gov/articles/PMC4360124/
5. 'Antonie van Leeuwenhoek', Britannica, https://www.britannica.com/biography/Antonie-van-Leeuwenhoek
6. 'Bastogne "Nuts!" Anthony McAuliffe', WW2 on Deadline, https://ww2ondeadline.substack.com/p/bastogne-nuts-anthony-mcauliffe
7. 'Battle of the Bulge: A Montana Perspective on the 80th Anniversary', Montana Military Museum, https://montanamilitarymuseum.org/fw-battle-of-the-bulge-a-montana-perspective-on-the-80th-anniversary/
8. 'Battle of the Bulge', https://encyclopedia.ushmm.org/content/en/article/battle-of-the-bulge
9. 'Battle of the Bulge', National WWII Museum, https://www.nationalww2museum.org/war/topics/battle-bulge
10. 'Battle of the Bulge', U.S. Army, https://www.army.mil/botb/
11. 'Framingham's Battle of the Bulge Veterans', Framingham History, https://framinghamhistory.org/framinghams-battle-of-the-bulge-veterans/
12. 'General Anthony C. McAuliffe', https://armyhistory.org/general-anthony-c-mcauliffe/
13. 'Germany Prepared for the Bulge', War History Online, https://www.warhistoryonline.com/instant-articles/germany-prepared-bulge.html
14. 'Hidden Stories of the Battle of the Bulge', Beaches of Normandy Tours, https://www.beachesofnormandy.com/articles/Hidden_stories_of_the_Battle_of_the_Bulge/?id=f11ebf5188
15. 'Hooke's Micrographia 1665', Cabinet Office Oxford, https://www.cabinet.ox.ac.uk/hookes-micrographia-1665-0
16. 'Koehler Illumination: A Brief History and a Practical Set-Up in Five Easy Steps', Leica Microsystems, https://www.leica-microsystems.com/science-lab/microscopy-basics/koehler-illumination-a-brief-history-and-a-practical-set-up-in-five-easy-steps/

NOTES

17. 'Köhler Illumination', Britannica,
https://www.britannica.com/technology/Kohler-illumination

18. 'Micrographia Under the Microscope', University of Glasgow Library Blog,
https://universityofglasgowlibrary.wordpress.com/2015/10/27/micrographia-under-the-microscope/

19. 'Micrographia, or Some Physiological Descriptions of Minute Bodies Made by Magnifying Glasses', Royal Collection Trust,
https://www.rct.uk/collection/1090263/micrographia-or-some-physiological-descriptions-of-minute-bodies-made-by

20. 'Micrographia', The Huntington,
https://www.huntington.org/digital-classroom-resources/micrographia

21. 'Micrographia', Wadham College Library,
https://library.wadham.ox.ac.uk/micrographia.html

22. 'NPR Story on the End of the Line at NUMMI', Lean Blog,
https://www.leanblog.org/2010/03/npr-story-on-the-end-of-the-line-at-nummi/

23. 'NUMMI 2015', This American Life,
https://www.thisamericanlife.org/561/nummi-2015

24. 'NUMMI', Marshall USC,
https://faculty.marshall.usc.edu/Paul-Adler/research/NUMMI%20ROB.pdf

25. 'Operation Watch am Rhein', Normandy American Heroes,
https://www.normandyamericanheroes.com/blog/blog-2/operation-watch-am-rhein

26. 'Parts', Lens on Leeuwenhoek,
https://lensonleeuwenhoek.net/content/parts

27. 'Pepys Diary Encyclopedia', Pepys Diary,
https://www.pepysdiary.com/encyclopedia/8180/

28. 'Popular Mechanics Article', Popular Mechanics,
https://www.popularmechanics.com/cars/a5514/4350856/

29. 'Reasons', University of Texas,
https://www.laits.utexas.edu/~anorman/long.extra/Projects.F97/GM/Reasons.html

30. 'Restoration Reading', The Royal Society,
https://royalsociety.org/blog/2013/04/restoration-reading/

31. 'Robert Hooke's Micrographia', Magdalene College Cambridge,
https://www.magd.cam.ac.uk/library-news/robert-hookes-micrographia-pl-2116

32. 'Surrender? Nuts! Gen. Anthony McAuliffe's 1944 Christmas Message to Troops',
https://archivesfoundation.org/documents/surrender-nuts-gen-anthony-mcauliffes-1944-christmas-message-troops/

33. 'The 17th-Century Cloth Merchant Who Discovered the Vast Realm of Tiny Microbes: An Appreciation of Antonie van Leeuwenhoek', The Conversation,
https://theconversation.com/the-17th-century-cloth-merchant-who-discovered-the-vast-realm-of-tiny-microbes-an-appreciation-of-antonie-van-leeuwenhoek-158177

34. 'The 17th-Century Cloth Merchant Who Discovered the Vast Realm of Tiny Microbes', ASBMB Today, https://www.asbmb.org/asbmb-today/people/050221/the-17th-century-cloth-merchant-who-discovered-the
35. 'The Battle of the Bulge at 70 Years', National Archives, https://www.archives.gov/publications/prologue/2014/winter/battle-of-the-bulge-70-years
36. 'The Micrographia Microscope', Science Museum, https://blog.sciencemuseum.org.uk/the-micrographia-microscope/
37. 'The Miracle, the Betrayal of NUMMI', WitnessLA, https://witnessla.com/the-miracle-the-betrayal-of-nummi/
38. 'The Rise and Fall of the Toyota-General Motors Joint Venture', Carbuzz, https://carbuzz.com/rise-and-fall-toyota-general-motors-joint-venture/
39. 'The Story of the "Nuts!" Reply', U.S. Army, https://www.army.mil/article/92856/the_story_of_the_nuts_reply
40. 'This American Life: NUMMI 2015', Ethics and Education, https://ethicsandeducation.wceruw.org/this-american-life-nummi-2015/
41. 'Understanding Illumination', Quekett Microscopical Club, https://www.quekett.org/resources/understanding/illumination
42. 'What We Can Learn from the Lean Car Plant', https://athena.ecs.csus.edu/~buckley/CSc170_F2018_files/
43. 'What You Need to Know About the Battle of the Bulge', Imperial War Museums, https://www.iwm.org.uk/history/what-you-need-to-know-about-the-battle-of-the-bulge

NOTES

Causal Model: Explanatory Precision

1. 'Hyman G. Rickover', Atomic Heritage Foundation, https://ahf.nuclearmuseum.org/ahf/profile/hyman-g-rickover/
2. 'Tycho Brahe', All That's Interesting, https://allthatsinteresting.com/tycho-brahe
3. 'The Astronomers Tycho Brahe and Johannes Kepler', Chandra X-Ray Observatory, https://chandra.harvard.edu/edu/formal/icecore/The_Astronomers_Tycho_Brahe_and_Johannes_Kepler.pdf
4. 'Tycho Brahe: The Scandalous Astronomer', TED-Ed, https://ed.ted.com/lessons/tycho-brahe-the-scandalous-astronomer-dan-wenkel/digdeeper
5. 'The Never-Ending Challenge of Engineering: Admiral H.G. Rickover in His Own Words', Engineering Management Institute, https://engineeringmanagementinstitute.org/tecc-92-the-never-ending-challenge-of-engineering-admiral-h-g-rickover-in-his-own-words/
6. 'Astronomer Tycho Brahe Was Born 460 Years Ago', Radio Prague International, https://english.radio.cz/astronomer-tycho-brahe-was-born-460-years-ago-8612823
7. 'Tycho Brahe', Northwestern University, https://faculty.wcas.northwestern.edu/infocom/Ideas/brahe.html
8. 'Johannes Kepler', The Galileo Project, https://galileo.library.rice.edu/sci/kepler.html
9. 'Tycho Brahe', Galileo and Einstein, https://galileoandeinstein.phys.virginia.edu/1995/lectures/tychob.html
10. 'Tycho Brahe', Galileo and Einstein, https://galileoandeinstein.phys.virginia.edu/1995/lectures/tychob.html
11. 'Tycho Brahe Collection', University of Arizona Libraries, https://lib.arizona.edu/special-collections/collections/tycho-brahe-collection
12. 'Of Dwarves, Pet Elk, and Gold Noses: Tycho Brahe, Danish Astronomer', Maidens and Manuscripts, https://maidensandmanuscripts.com/2019/12/29/of-dwarves-pet-elk-and-gold-noses-tycho-brahe-danish-astronomer/
13. 'Johannes Kepler', MacTutor History of Mathematics Archive, https://mathshistory.st-andrews.ac.uk/Biographies/Kepler/
14. 'Kepler's Laws', MacTutor History of Mathematics Archive, https://mathshistory.st-andrews.ac.uk/HistTopics/Keplers_laws/
15. 'Tycho Brahe', MacTutor History of Mathematics Archive, https://mathshistory.st-andrews.ac.uk/SH/brahe_sh.pdf
16. 'Johannes Kepler and the New Astronomy', Taylor University, https://pillars.taylor.edu/cgi/viewcontent.cgi?article=1000&context=acmsjournal-2008-09

17. 'Rickover Interview', Salt for Sermons,
https://saltforsermons.org.uk/rickover-interview/
18. 'Planetary Motion', NASA Science,
https://science.nasa.gov/earth/earth-observatory/planetary-motion/
19. 'Orbits and Kepler's Laws', NASA Science,
https://science.nasa.gov/solar-system/orbits-and-keplers-laws/
20. 'Interview Techniques', SJL,
https://sjl.us/tag/interview-techniques/
21. 'Jepp Who Defied the Stars', The Appendix,
https://theappendix.net/issues/2013/4/fiction-jepp-who-defied-the-stars
22. 'The Invention of Data', The Data Generalist,
https://thedatageneralist.com/the-invention-of-data/
23. '400 Years of the Third Law: An Overlooked and Neglected Revolution in Astronomy', Thony C's Blog,
https://thonyc.wordpress.com/2018/05/15/400-years-of-the-third-law-an-overlooked-and-neglected-revolution-in-astronomy/
24. 'The Emergence of Modern Astronomy: A Complex Mosaic Part XII', Thony C's Blog,
https://thonyc.wordpress.com/2019/06/05/the-emergence-of-modern-astronomy-a-complex-mosaic-part-xii/
25. 'RCL John Sheehan', USS Rickover,
https://ussrickover.org/rcl-john-sheehan/
26. 'Tycho's Data', INFN National Laboratories of Frascati,
https://w3.lnf.infn.it/tychos-data/?lang=en
27. 'Tycho Brahe's Moose', Ancient Origins,
https://www.ancient-origins.net/weird-facts/tycho-brahes-moose-0019454
28. 'Johannes Kepler', Britannica,
https://www.britannica.com/biography/Johannes-Kepler
29. 'Tycho Brahe', Britannica,
https://www.britannica.com/biography/Tycho-Brahe-Danish-astronomer
30. 'Tycho, Kepler, and Galileo', Britannica,
https://www.britannica.com/science/history-of-science/Tycho-Kepler-and-Galileo
31. 'Tychonic System', Britannica,
https://www.britannica.com/science/Tychonic-system
32. 'Understanding Kepler's Laws of Planetary Motion', Britannica,
https://www.britannica.com/story/understanding-keplers-laws-of-planetary-motion
33. 'Uraniborg', Britannica,
https://www.britannica.com/topic/Uraniborg
34. 'Johannes Kepler (1571–1630): His Life & Work', BRLSI,
https://www.brlsi.org/whatson/johannes-kepler-1571-1630-his-life-work/

NOTES

35. 'Kepler's Three Laws: Second Astronomical Revolution', Cabinet Office Oxford, https://www.cabinet.ox.ac.uk/keplers-three-laws-second-astronomical-revolution
36. 'Tycho Brahe: Astronomer and Alchemist at the Court of Rudolf II', Café Boheme, https://www.cafeboheme.cz/tycho-brahe-astronomer-and-alchemist-at-the-court-of-rudolf-ii/
37. 'Kepler's Laws of Planetary Motion, 1609–1666', Cambridge University Press, https://www.cambridge.org/core/journals/british-journal-for-the-history-of-science/article/abs/keplers-laws-of-planetary-motion-16091666/699210848492633F05BA8C2BC2790EF2
38. 'Tycho Brahe', EBSCO Research Starters, https://www.ebsco.com/research-starters/history/tycho-brahe
39. 'The Astronomer's Nose: Tycho Brahe's Controversial Prosthesis', ENT & Audiology News, https://www.entandaudiologynews.com/features/ent-features/post/the-astronomer-s-nose-tycho-brahe-s-controversial-prosthesis
40. 'Tycho Brahe and Early Modern Astronomy', Frontiers in Astronomy and Space Sciences, https://www.frontiersin.org/journals/astronomy-and-space-sciences/articles/10.3389/fspas.2023.1255481/full
41. 'The History of Johannes Kepler', Jet Propulsion Laboratory, https://www.jpl.nasa.gov/news/the-history-of-johannes-kepler/
42. 'Tycho Brahe's Astronomical Observations: Precision Without Telescopes', Kronecker Wallis, https://www.kroneckerwallis.com/tycho-brahes-astronomical-observations-precision-without-telescopes/
43. 'The World's Fabric', Linda Hall Library, https://www.lindahall.org/about/news/the-worlds-fabric/
44. 'Whose Revolution? Copernicus, Brahe, and Kepler', Library of Congress, https://www.loc.gov/static/collections/finding-our-place-in-the-cosmos-with-carl-sagan/articles-and-essays/modeling-the-cosmos/whose-revolution-copernicus-brahe-and-kepler.html
45. 'Kepler', Purdue University, https://www.math.purdue.edu/-eremenko/dvi/kepler.pdf
46. 'Tycho Brahe', NJRS, https://www.njrs.dk/12_2017/10_oestermark_brahe.pdf
47. 'Brahe', University of Rochester, https://www.pas.rochester.edu/~blackman/ast104/brahe10.html
48. 'Rickover', Rickover, https://www.rickover.com
49. 'Biography', University of Rostock, https://www.uni-rostock.de/en/university/history/anniversary-of-the-university-2019/information/tycho-brahe-exhibition/biography/
50. 'Stories About Retired Adm. Hyman Rickover Abound', UPI, https://www.upi.com/Archives/1986/07/08/Stories-about-retired-Adm-Hyman-Rickover-abound-tales/4882521179200/

51. 'Passing Rickover's Muster', U.S. Naval Institute, https://www.usni.org/magazines/naval-history-magazine/1992/march/passing-rickovers-muster
52. 'Hyman G. Rickover', U.S. Naval Institute, https://www.usni.org/people/hyman-g-rickover
53. *Ne frustra vixisse videar*: Documented in Kepler's own first-hand account of Brahe's final days, as cited in J.L.E. Dreyer, *Tycho Brahe: A Picture of Scientific Life and Work in the Sixteenth Century* (1890), Chapter 11. Also recorded in Wikipedia's entry on Tycho Brahe, citing the same primary source: 'The night before he died, he suffered from a delirium during which he was frequently heard to exclaim that he hoped he would not seem to have lived in vain.'
54. The Nokia CEO's quote ('Being fast is significantly more important than foreseeing what happens in the market. This is our key competitive advantage.'): Attributed to CEO Olli-Pekka Kallasvuo, *Suomen Kuvalehti*, issue 10/2006, as cited and translated in: Lamberg, J.-A., Lubinaité, S., Ojala, J., and Tikkanen, H., 'The Curse of Agility: The Nokia Corporation and the Loss of Market Dominance in Mobile Phones, 2003–2013', Business History vol. 63, no. 4 (2021), Taylor and Francis. The quote appears in Finnish in the source; the English translation is as rendered in Lamberg et al.
55. Nokia smartphone market share figures: IDC data, as cited in multiple academic and industry sources. Nokia's global smartphone share was approximately 50.8% in Q2 2007, falling to approximately 3.1% by Q2 2013.
56. Nokia's internal strategic culture and the Japan research centre: Lamberg et al. (2021), drawing on oral history interviews with Nokia managers and executives.
57. Rickover selection process: Documented in Naval History Magazine, Spring 1992, Vol. 6, No. 1, 'Passing Rickover's Muster,' US Naval Institute. Multiple first-hand accounts are also available in the US Naval Institute archive and the Rickover Papers collection.

NOTES

Coupling Architecture: Cross-System Loops

1. 'The Song Dynasty in China', Asia for Educators, https://afe.easia.columbia.edu/songdynasty-module/index.html
2. 'Song Dynasty', Smithsonian Institution, https://asia-archive.si.edu/learn/for-educators/teaching-china-with-the-smithsonian/explore-by-dynasty/song-dynasty/
3. 'Chola Dynasty', Smithsonian Institution, https://asia-archive.si.edu/learn/india-shiva-nataraja-lord-of-the-dance/chola-dynasty/
4. 'Research on the Economic Development of the Song Dynasty', Frontiers in Business, Economics and Management, https://drpress.org/ojs/index.php/fbem/article/view/7455/7248
5. 'The Chola Empire and Women in History', Frontline, https://frontline.thehindu.com/books/chola-empire-women-history-lords-of-earth-and-sea-excerpt-anirudh-kanisetti/article69112728.ece
6. 'The Song Dynasty', History Guild, https://historyguild.org/the-song-dynasty/
7. 'Fiscal and Economic Policies in the Song Dynasty', Frontiers of History in China, https://journal.hep.com.cn/fhc/EN/10.3868/s020-013-024-0019-6
8. 'Reading the Cholas Right', Open Magazine, https://openthemagazine.com/lounge/books/reading-the-cholas-right
9. 'How Rajendra Chola and His Army Sailed Across the Seas in the 11th Century', Scroll.in, https://scroll.in/article/1078060/how-rajendra-chola-and-his-army-sailed-across-the-seas-in-the-11th-century-to-beat-the-malaysians
10. 'Mare Nostrum', University of Texas, https://sites.utexas.edu/culturescontexts/tag/mare-nostrum/
11. 'Introduction to the Song Dynasty', Smarthistory, https://smarthistory.org/song-dynasty-intro/
12. 'Anirudh Kanisetti on Lords of Earth and Sea', TamilCulture, https://tamilculture.com/anirudh-kanisetti-on-lords-of-earth-and-sea-a-history-of-the-chola-empire
13. 'A Medieval Malayan King Beat Cholas at Their Game', ThePrint, https://theprint.in/opinion/a-medieval-malayan-king-beat-cholas-at-their-game-almost-created-a-superpower/1425362/
14. 'Extensive and Sometimes Mythical History of the Chola Empire', Ancient Origins, https://www.ancient-origins.net/ancient-places-asia/extensive-and-sometimes-mythical-history-chola-empire-005613
15. 'BBC News Article', BBC News, https://www.bbc.com/news/articles/cm27zn0vl33o
16. 'How China's Song Dynasty Changed the World', BBC News Magazine, https://www.bbc.com/news/magazine-19962432

17. 'Wang Anshi', Britannica,
https://www.britannica.com/biography/Wang-Anshi
18. 'Chola Dynasty', Britannica,
https://www.britannica.com/topic/Chola-dynasty
19. 'Song Dynasty', Britannica,
https://www.britannica.com/topic/Song-dynasty
20. 'The Song Dynasty', China Highlights,
https://www.chinahighlights.com/travelguide/china-history/the-song-dynasty.htm
21. 'Science and Technology in the Song Dynasty', EBSCO Research Starters,
https://www.ebsco.com/research-starters/history/science-and-technology-song-dynasty
22. 'Wang Anshi Introduces Bureaucratic Reforms', EBSCO Research Starters,
https://www.ebsco.com/research-starters/history/wang-anshi-introduces-bureaucratic-reforms
23. 'The Real Reason Why the Cholas Invaded Kedah's Waters', Free Malaysia Today,
https://www.freemalaysiatoday.com/category/leisure/2021/07/28/the-real-reason-why-the-cholas-invaded-kedahs-waters
24. 'The Indian Lords of Trade', Live History India,
https://www.livehistoryindia.com/story/eras/the-indian-lords-of-trade
25. 'The Southern Song Dynasty (1127–1279)', The Metropolitan Museum of Art,
https://www.metmuseum.org/essays/southern-song-dynasty-1127-1279
26. 'Gangaikondacholapuram and the Chola Dynasty', National Geographic,
https://www.nationalgeographic.com/travel/article/gangaikondacholapuram-southern-india-chola-dynasty-ponniyin-selvan-1
27. 'Do Cholas Belong to Hindus?', Newslaundry,
https://www.newslaundry.com/2025/03/03/do-cholas-belong-to-hindus-anirudh-kanisetti-on-why-theres-no-point-trying-to-claim-them
28. 'How China's Song Dynasty Was a Great Time for the Nation but Terrible for Many Women', South China Morning Post,
https://www.scmp.com/lifestyle/chinese-culture/article/3330195/how-chinas-song-dynasty-was-great-time-nation-terrible-one-many-women
29. 'Song Dynasty: A Brief History', TheCollector,
https://www.thecollector.com/song-dynasty-brief-history/
30. 'Song Dynasty', University of Tennessee at Chattanooga,
https://www.utc.edu/health-education-and-professional-studies/asia-program/2018-ncta-teaching-modules/song-dynasty
31. 'Song Dynasty', World History Encyclopedia,
https://www.worldhistory.org/Song_Dynasty/
32. *Lords of Earth and Sea: A History of the Chola Empire*, Juggernaut, Anirudh Kanisetti (2025).
33. Kanisetti, Anirudh (2025). *Lords of Earth and Sea: A History of the Chola Empire. Juggernaut.*

NOTES

Decision Clock Speed: Causal Decentralization

1. 'An African Slave Who Defied the Mughals', Manu S. Pillai, https://manuspillai.com/2019/12/13/an-african-slave-who-defied-the-mughals-14-december-2019/
2. 'Book Review', World History Connected / George Mason University Journals, https://journals.gmu.edu/whc/article/view/4049/2255
3. 'Malik Ambar (1548–1626): The Rise and Fall of Military Slavery', Cambridge University Press, https://www.cambridge.org/core/books/abs/social-history-of-the-deccan-13001761/malik-ambar-15481626-the-rise-and-fall-of-military-slavery/4513E28350A64CDE4F1A1DE54059896F
4. 'Malik Ambar (1548–1626)', BlackPast, https://blackpast.org/global-african-history/ambar-malik-1548-1626/
5. 'Malik Ambar [PDF]', Columbia University South Asia Institute, https://sai.columbia.edu/sites/sai.columbia.edu/files/content/Ali%20-%20Malik%20Ambar.pdf
6. 'Malik Ambar: A Remarkable Life', Everything Harar, https://everythingharar.com/malik-ambar-a-remarkable-life/
7. 'Malik Ambar: The African Slave Who Took on the Mughals', TRT World, https://www.trtworld.com/article/12733775?_rt=1
8. 'Malik Ambar', BBC, https://www.bbc.com/audio/play/b05wy644
9. 'The Ethiopian Ruler of Maharashtra', Deccan Heritage Foundation, https://www.deccan-heritage-foundation.org/travel-notes/the-ethiopian-ruler-of-maharashtra/
10. 'The Slave Who Built a City', Sarmaya, https://sarmaya.in/reads/slave-who-built-a-city/
11. 'The Story of Malik Ambar [PDF]', FirstRand, https://www.firstrand.co.za/media/new-articles/the-story-of-malika-ambar.pdf
12. 'What Does the Legacy of Malik Ambar Tell Us About the African-Origin Diaspora in India?', IMPART, https://imp-art.org/perspectives/dispatches/what-does-the-legacy-of-malik-ambar-tell-us-about-the-african-origin-diaspora-in-india/
13. 'Who Was Malik Ambar? The African Slave Turned Mercenary Kingmaker', TheCollector, https://www.thecollector.com/who-is-malik-ambar-african-slave-turned-mercenary-kingmaker/

System Architecture: Stable Interface

1. 'Maharaja Ranjit Singh's Americans', American Turban, https://americanturban.com/2013/10/24/maharaja-ranjit-singhs-americans/
2. 'Lidl ERP Failure: SAP Retail Case Study', ERP Perspective, https://erpperspective.com/blogs/real-world-stories/lidl-erp-failure-sap-retail-case-study
3. 'Arm Releasing First In-House Chip', Yahoo Finance, https://finance.yahoo.com/sectors/technology/articles/arm-releasing-first-house-chip-194854816.html?guccounter=1
4. 'Meet VW's Secret Weapon', Fortune, https://fortune.com/2012/04/19/meet-vws-secret-weapon/
5. 'German Giant Lidl's Six-Year Bid to Switch to SAP Fails', iTWire, https://itwire.com/enterprise-solutions/german-giant-lidl-s-six-year-bid-to-switch-to-sap-fails
6. 'Ranjit Singh: Sikh Warrior King', The Past, https://the-past.com/review/whats-on/ranjit-singh-sikh-warrior-king/
7. 'The Napoleon of the Punjab', The Lamp Magazine, https://thelampmagazine.com/issues/issue-25/the-napoleon-of-the-punjab
8. 'Soldier and Traveller: Memoirs of Alexander Gardner [PDF]', Wikimedia Commons, https://upload.wikimedia.org/wikipedia/commons/3/33/Soldier_and_traveller%3B_memoirs_of_Alexander_Gardner%2C_Colonel_of_Artillery_in_the_service_of_Maharaja_Ranjit_Singh_%28IA_soldiertraveller00gardiala%29.pdf
9. 'Ranjit Singh Has Been Likened to Mehmet Ali', Wunderkammer Tales, https://wunderkammertales.blogspot.com/2015/06/ranjit-singh-has-been-likened-to-mehmet.html
10. 'TSMC: The Most Important Company in the World', ABC News Australia, https://www.abc.net.au/news/2023-08-19/tsmc-the-most-important-company-in-the-world/102728172
11. 'TSMC', Acquired Podcast, https://www.acquired.fm/episodes/tsmc
12. 'Volkswagen Group's MQB Platform Explained', autoevolution, https://www.autoevolution.com/news/volkswagen-group-s-mqb-platform-explained-78771.html
13. 'VW's Platforms to Perform', Automotive Manufacturing Solutions, https://www.automotivemanufacturingsolutions.com/strategy/vws-platforms-to-perform/541419
14. 'Morris Chang', Britannica, https://www.britannica.com/money/Morris-Chang
15. 'Volkswagen's Cost-Slashing MQB Passes Milestone', CarExpert, https://www.carexpert.com.au/car-news/volkswagens-cost-slashing-mqb-passes-milestone
16. 'Arm Wants a Bigger Slice of the Chip Business', The Economist, https://www.economist.com/business/2026/02/12/arm-wants-a-bigger-slice-of-the-chip-business

NOTES

17. 'Case Study 12: Lidl's €500 Million SAP Debacle', Henrico Dolfing, https://www.henricodolfing.ch/en/case-study-12-lidls-e500-million-sap-debacle/
18. 'Ranjit Singh's French Connection', Live History India, https://www.livehistoryindia.com/story/people/ranjit-singhs-french-connection
19. 'The Semiconductor Founding Father', NPR, https://www.npr.org/2021/12/21/1066548023/the-semiconductor-founding-father
20. 'The Chip Titan Whose Life's Work Is at the Center of a Tech Cold War', The New York Times, https://www.nytimes.com/2023/08/04/technology/the-chip-titan-whose-lifes-work-is-at-the-center-of-a-tech-cold-war.html
21. 'Arm Holdings to Sell Chips', The New York Times, https://www.nytimes.com/2026/03/24/technology/arm-holdings-sell-chips.html
22. 'Lidl's Failed IT Project Cost Half a Billion', RetailDetail, https://www.retaildetail.eu/news/food/lidls-failed-it-project-cost-half-billion/
23. 'Has Volkswagen Discovered the Holy Grail of Carmakers?', Reuters, https://www.reuters.com/article/business/has-volkswagen-discovered-the-holy-grail-of-car-makers-idUSBRE91A04D/
24. 'General Jean-François Allard With His Family in Lahore', Sotheby's, https://www.sothebys.com/en/buy/auction/2023/the-edith-stuart-cary-welch-collection-part-iii/general-jean-francois-allard-with-his-family-in
25. 'Arm Is Making Its Own Chips for the First Time', Telecoms.com, https://www.telecoms.com/digital-ecosystem/arm-is-making-its-own-chips-for-the-first-time
26. 'Arm Looks to Launch Its Own Chip After Landing Meta Contract', The Guardian, https://www.theguardian.com/business/2025/feb/14/arm-looks-to-launch-its-own-chip-after-landing-meta-contract
27. 'Volkswagen Group Taps Into New Profit Pools With Sustainable Mobility', Volkswagen Group, https://www.volkswagen-group.com/en/press-releases/volkswagen-group-taps-into-new-profit-pools-with-sustainable-mobility-17606
28. 'Volkswagen Group MQB Milestone', Volkswagen UK Press, https://www.vwpress.co.uk/releases/4794
29. 'Ranjit Singh's Army: His Firangis', Wallace Collection, https://www.wallacecollection.org/explore/explore-in-depth/the-sikh-empire/sikh-arms-armour/ranjit-singhs-army-his-firangis/
30. 'Chip Design Firm Arm Is Making Its Own AI CPU', Wired, https://www.wired.com/story/chip-design-firm-arm-is-making-its-own-ai-cpu/
31. 'Haribo, Lidl, Deutsche Post and Co.: The Long List of Difficult and Failed SAP Projects', WirtschaftsWoche, https://www.wiwo.de/unternehmen/it/haribo-lidl-deutsche-post-und-co-die-lange-liste-schwieriger-und-gefloppter-sap-projekte/23771296.html

Rule Architecture: Vacant Throne

1. 'Apple Made Secret 5-Year $275B Deal With Chinese Government', AppleInsider, https://appleinsider.com/articles/21/12/07/apple-made-secret-5-year-275b-deal-with-chinese-government
2. 'Patrick McGee: Apple in China', Asia Society, https://asiasociety.org/center-us-china-relations/events/patrick-mcgee-apple-china
3. 'Patrick McGee on Apple in China', Asia Society Video, https://asiasociety.org/video/patrick-mcgee-apple-china
4. 'Joux: A Place of Memories Past', Château de Joux, https://chateaudejoux.com/en/discover-the-chateau/joux-a-place-of-memories-past/
5. 'The Question of Power in Monsieur Toussaint and The Tragedy of King Christophe', eScholarship, https://escholarship.org/content/qt8d01x3d8/qt8d01x3d8.pdf
6. 'La Promesse Oubliée à Toussaint Louverture', Histoire Coloniale, https://histoirecoloniale.net/la-promesse-oubliee-a-toussaint-louverture/
7. 'Patrick McGee, Apple in China and...', Maven Maverick, https://mavenmaverick.substack.com/p/patrick-mcgee-apple-in-china-and
8. 'Toussaint Louverture', National Museum of African American History and Culture, https://nmaahc.si.edu/latinx/toussaint-louverture
9. 'Visa', Spotify, https://open.spotify.com/episode/6DHmmmJX2ATX6MTBEuwbFa
10. 'The Insurers Who Always Paid Out: The Lloyd's of London Story', Apple Podcasts, https://podcasts.apple.com/de/podcast/the-insurers-who-always-paid-out-the-lloyds-of/id1844409167?i=1000758254430
11. 'Petion, Dessaline, Toussaint Louverture 1801-1803 ; Expédition de Saint -Domingue 1801-1803', Ministère de la Culture (France), https://pop.culture.gouv.fr/notice/joconde/00640040194
12. 'Toussaint Louverture', Slavery and Remembrance, https://slaveryandremembrance.org/people/person/?id=PP052
13. 'What Did Apple Get Out of Its Secret $275 Billion China Deal in 2016?', The China Project, https://thechinaproject.com/2021/12/07/what-did-apple-get-out-of-its-secret-275-billion-china-deal-in-2016/
14. 'Visa', Acquired Podcast, https://www.acquired.fm/episodes/visa
15. 'Toussaint L'Ouverture: Hero of the Haitian slave rebellion', BBC, https://www.bbc.com/audio/play/w3cszjwn
16. 'The Coffee House: A Brief History', Berrys Coffee House, https://www.berryscoffeehouse.co.uk/the-coffee-house-a-brief-history/
17. 'Toussaint Louverture', Britannica, https://www.britannica.com/biography/Toussaint-Louverture

NOTES

18. 'Lloyd's', Britannica,
https://www.britannica.com/money/Lloyds

19. 'Toussaint Louverture, the Cultivator System, and Haiti's Independence, 1798–1804', Cambridge University Press,
https://www.cambridge.org/core/books/abs/cambridge-history-of-the-age-of-atlantic-revolutions/toussaint-louverture-the-cultivator-system-and-haitis-independence-17981804/4FC3B7C38A071519A0B45A363DA52331

20. 'The Cessation of Zheng He's Voyages and the Beginning of Private Sailings', Journal of Chinese History,
https://www.cambridge.org/core/journals/journal-of-chinese-history/article/cessation-of-zheng-hes-voyages-and-the-beginning-of-private-sailings-fiscal-competition-between-emperors-and-bureaucrats/8FE45F3210A4DF174A4EC2B30868D433

21. 'Apple Invested at Least $275 Billion in China Since 2016', CNET,
https://www.cnet.com/tech/mobile/apple-invested-at-least-275-billion-in-china-since-2016-according-to-new-report/

22. 'Wars of Toussaint Louverture', EBSCO,
https://www.ebsco.com/research-starters/history/wars-toussaint-louverture

23. '1801: Hyacinth Moïse, Haitian Revolution General', Executed Today,
https://www.executedtoday.com/2020/11/09/1801-hyacinth-moise-haitian-revolution-general/

24. 'The Trillion-Dollar Vision of Dee Hock', Fast Company,
https://www.fastcompany.com/27333/trillion-dollar-vision-dee-hock

25. 'Apple's $275 Billion China Bet Is Now a Major Risk', Forbes,
https://www.forbes.com/sites/stevebanker/2025/08/02/apples-275-billion-china-bet-is-now-a-major-risk/

26. 'Lloyd's of London: Failure in the Market', Stanford Graduate School of Business,
https://www.gsb.stanford.edu/faculty-research/case-studies/lloyds-london-failure-market

27. 'A Statue of Toussaint Louverture Unveiled at La Rochelle', Haiti Libre,
https://www.haitilibre.com/en/news-13941-haiti-culture-a-statue-of-toussaint-louverture-unveiled-at-la-rochelle.html

28. 'Visa CEO History', History Oasis,
https://www.historyoasis.com/post/visa-ceo-history

29. 'The Wrongful Death of Toussaint Louverture', History Today,
https://www.historytoday.com/archive/feature/wrongful-death-toussaint-louverture

30. 'How iPhones Built a Superpower', Hoover Institution,
https://www.hoover.org/research/how-iphones-built-superpower-patrick-mcgee

31. 'Toussaint Louverture - Jean-Jacques Dessalines rupture ou continuité?', Le National,
https://www.lenational.org/post_article.php?tri=323

32. 'History of Lloyd's', Lloyd's,
https://www.lloyds.com/about-lloyds/history

33. 'Coffee and Commerce', Lloyd's,
https://www.lloyds.com/about-lloyds/history/coffee-and-commerce

34. 'Edward Lloyd', Lloyd's,
https://www.lloyds.com/about-lloyds/history/important-people-from-our-past/edward-lloyd

35. 'Our Past and Present', Lloyd's,
https://www.lloyds.com/about-lloyds/join-lloyds-market/sales-enablement-hub/why-lloyds/our-past-and-present

36. 'Black Spartacus: The Epic Life of Toussaint Louverture', Napoleon.org,
https://www.napoleon.org/en/magazine/publications/black-spartacus-the-epic-life-of-toussaint-louverture/

37. 'Toussaint Louverture: The Liberator of Santo Domingo', New York Times,
https://www.nytimes.com/1931/04/05/archives/toussaint-louverture-the-liberator-of-santo-domingo-toussaint.html

38. 'Toussaint Louverture', Perspective Media,
https://www.perspectivemedia.com/toussaint-louverture/

39. 'The Insurers Who Always Paid Out: The Lloyd's of London Story, Part I', Pushkin FM,
https://www.pushkin.fm/podcasts/business-history/the-insurers-who-always-paid-out-the-lloyds-of-london-story-part-i

40. 'Apple's Ugly China Deal Mostly Bought Time', Reuters,
https://www.reuters.com/breakingviews/apples-ugly-china-deal-mostly-bought-time-2021-12-08/

41. 'Apple's Ugly China Deal Mostly Bought Time', Reuters,
https://www.reuters.com/breakingviews/apples-ugly-china-deal-mostly-bought-time-2021-12-08/

42. 'Haiti's Black Spartacus: Toussaint Louverture and Abolishing Slavery', The Africa Report,
https://www.theafricareport.com/47223/haitis-black-spartacus-toussaint-louverture-and-abolishing-slavery/

43. 'Zheng He and the Closing of Ming China', TheCollector,
https://www.thecollector.com/zheng-he-closing-ming-china/

44. 'Black Spartacus Review: Superb History of Haiti', The Guardian,
https://www.theguardian.com/books/2020/oct/11/black-spartacus-the-epic-life-of-toussaint-louverture-review-superb-history-of-haiti

45. 'Apple China Deal: Tim Cook and the $275bn Bargain', The Guardian,
https://www.theguardian.com/technology/2021/dec/07/apple-china-deal-tim-cook

46. 'The Seven Voyages of the Treasure Fleet', ThoughtCo,
https://www.thoughtco.com/the-seven-voyages-of-the-treasure-fleet-195215

47. 'Understanding Insurance: What Is Lloyd's of London?', Vertafore,
https://www.vertafore.com/resources/blog/understanding-insurance-what-lloyds-london

48. 'Part 5: Visa Founder and CEO Dee Hock: One from Many: VISA and the Rise of Chaordic Organisation', YouTube, https://www.youtube.com/watch?v=_29umUkGUTc
49. 'How a Coffee Shop Became the Most Powerful Insurance Empire on Earth', YouTube, https://www.youtube.com/watch?v=YJ9QN5E-jlsfdc0eb

Trusted Network: Verified Threshold

1. 'The Champagne Fairs', Vieux Troyes, http://vieuxtroyes.free.fr/t/engfoires.htm
2. 'The Medieval Champagne Fairs: Lessons for Development', CEPR VoxEU, https://cepr.org/voxeu/columns/medieval-champagne-fairs-lessons-development
3. 'Teach Me How to Shruggie', Pluralistic / Cory Doctorow, https://doctorow.medium.com/https-pluralistic-net-2024-04-04-teach-me-how-to-shruggie-kagi-caaa88c221f2
4. 'The Hanseatic League', History of the Germans, https://historyofthegermans.com/hanseatic-league/
5. 'Hanseatic League History & Civilization', Chalmers University of Technology Research, https://research.chalmers.se/publication/528778/file/528778_Fulltext.pdf
6. 'History', Rheinische Hanse, https://rheinischehanse.de/en/history/
7. 'Hanseatic League', Cultures and Contexts (UT Austin), https://sites.utexas.edu/culturescontexts/tag/hanseatic-league/
8. 'The Rise and Fall of the Hanseatic League', Works in Progress, https://worksinprogress.co/issue/the-rise-and-fall-of-the-hanseatic-league/
9. 'The Hanseatic League', BBC News, https://www.bbc.co.uk/news/extra/A2MFANtn3Z/hanseatic_league
10. 'Champagne Fair', Britannica, https://www.britannica.com/topic/Champagne-Fair
11. 'Hanseatic League', Britannica, https://www.britannica.com/topic/Hanseatic-League
12. 'Berkshire Hathaway Annual Meeting Draws Thousands', CBS News, https://www.cbsnews.com/news/berkshire-hathaway-annual-meeting-warren-buffet-profits-shareholders/
13. 'Bar-sur-Aube Champagne Fairs', Champagne Patrimoine Mondial, https://www.champagne-patrimoinemondial.org/en/decouvrir/bar-sur-aube-champagne-fairs-champagne-bubbles
14. 'The History of the Berkshire Hathaway Annual Meeting', Forbes, https://www.forbes.com/sites/robertdaugherty/2025/05/02/the-history-of-the-berkshire-hathaways-annual-meeting/
15. 'The Historical Hanse', Hansa Park, https://www.hansapark.de/die-historische-hanse?language=en
16. 'The Hanse', Hanse.org, https://www.hanse.org/en
17. 'The Medieval Hanseatic League', Hanse.org, https://www.hanse.org/en/the-medieval-hanseatic-league

NOTES

18. 'The Hanseatic League', Heritage History, https://www.heritage-history.com/index.php?c=read&author=colvin&book=germans&story=league

19. 'The Hanseatic League: Europe's First Common Market', History Today, https://www.historytoday.com/archive/feature/hanseatic-league-europes-first-common-market

20. 'What Lessons for Economic Development Can We Draw from the Champagne Fairs?', Ifo Institute, https://www.ifo.de/DocDL/cesifo1_wp3438.pdf

21. 'Inside the Berkshire Hathaway Annual Meeting', Investopedia, https://www.investopedia.com/inside-the-berkshire-hathaway-annual-meeting-5270517

22. 'The Medieval Champagne Fairs: A Crucible of Economic, Social and Political Change', I Take History, https://www.itakehistory.com/post/the-medieval-champagne-fairs-a-crucible-of-economic-social-and-political-change

23. 'Berkshire Hathaway at a Glance', Reuters, https://www.reuters.com/legal/transactional/berkshire-hathaway-glance-2026-04-30/

24. 'Hanseatic Period', UNESCO World Heritage Wismar-Stralsund, https://www.wismar-stralsund.de/en/world_heritage/history/hanseatic_period/

25. 'The History of Champagne', World History Encyclopedia, https://www.worldhistory.org/article/1913/the-history-of-champagne/

26. 'Hanseatic League', World History Encyclopedia, https://www.worldhistory.org/Hanseatic_League/

www.ingramcontent.com/pod-product-compliance
Lightning Source LLC
Chambersburg PA
CBHW071439230926
51846CB00001B/289
* 9 7 8 3 9 8 2 8 9 7 2 1 9 *